Praise for

Becoming a Badass

"Blessed with an indefatigable spirit, insatiable curiosity, and unquenchable zest for life, Margie Goldsmith shares her inspiring journey from humble beginnings to remarkable success as an award-winning writer, filmmaker, and novelist. In life and in love, she refuses to let fear hold her back from living the life she wanted, never settling for anything less—and urges all of us to do the same."

—Patrick Perry
Editor-in-Chief, *The Saturday Evening Post*

"Goldsmith's memoir is a full-throttle look at what happens when you decide to be unafraid in life. Born into a repressive family at a time when women were expected to get married and have a family, she rejects that model and decides to forge her own life; discovering sex, love, drugs, travel, and so much more. This book is a reminder that you can choose to live life on your own terms, building a career based on talent, passion, and enjoyment. More than anything, as a writer, it's a fun romp of a read—a romp through a woman's life that takes the reader from a repressive childhood to understanding an agency over her life. Using a garden metaphor, Goldsmith illustrates the awakening of a woman to herself, to love, ambition, and career, and most of all to contentment."

—Lee Woodruff
NYT Best-selling Author

"Some people never learn to roll with the punches, embrace adventure, and savor every minute of this precious life, but Margie Goldsmith seems to have done all this from an early age. As she notes in the preface of this hard-to-put-down memoir, she has faced formidable odds over the years, including a dysfunctional family, divorces, and health scares. But she has managed to endure, thrive, and remain optimistic while also visiting 150 countries on seven continents. Her colorful tale offers an entertaining read and important lessons for anyone who has faced challenges in life."

—Jeff Burger
Veteran Magazine Editor, Author of *Leonard Cohen on Leonard Cohen* and *Dylan on Dylan*

Becoming a Badass

From Fearful to Fierce

Becoming a Badass

From Fearful to Fierce

A Memoir

Margie Goldsmith

BOOKLOGIX®
Alpharetta, GA

The author has tried to recreate events, locations, and conversations from her memories of them. In some instances, in order to maintain their anonymity, the author has changed the names of individuals and places. She may also have changed some identifying characteristics and details such as physical attributes, occupations, and places of residence.

Copyright © 2025 by Margie Goldsmith

All rights reserved. No part of this book may be reproduced or transmitted in any form or by any means, electronic or mechanical, including photocopying, recording, or any information storage and retrieval system, without permission in writing from the author.

ISBN: 978-1-6653-1061-1 - Paperback
eISBN: 978-1-6653-1062-8 - eBook

These ISBNs are the property of BookLogix for the express purpose of sales and distribution of this title. The content of this book is the property of the copyright holder only. BookLogix does not hold any ownership of the content of this book and is not liable in any way for the materials contained within. The views and opinions expressed in this book are the property of the Author/Copyright holder, and do not necessarily reflect those of BookLogix.

Library of Congress Control Number: 2025916715

☉This paper meets the requirements of ANSI/NISO Z39.48-1992 (Permanence of Paper)

0 8 1 2 2 5

*This book is for anyone
who has ever felt not good enough.
You ARE good enough!*

Contents

Preface   ix

PART I

1. Hydrangea: Granny Elsa   3
2. Rose: My Mother   9
3. Yellow Carnation: My Father   15
4. Goutweed: My Older Sister   21
5. Lipstick Plant: My Younger Sister   27
6. Cobra Lily: Me, the Early Years   31
7. My High School Years   35
8. Bob, My First Boyfriend   41

PART II

9. Deciding to Live in Paris   53
10. Tiger Lily: Vincent   63
11. Chameleon: John   77
12. Life with John   85
13. The Big Change in John   93

14. Life on My Own	103
15. Outward Bound Changes My Life	111

PART III

16. The Good Life	121
17. Too Good to Be True	129
18. The Big Ditch	137
19. The Separation	147
20. Sunflower: Brian	157
21. Poppy: Hope	167
22. Changing My Life Again	175
23. Gardenia: JR	183
24. Bali and Beyond	193
25. Marital Problems and More Health Issues	201
26. My Life Today	209
Acknowledgments	217

Preface

Families are the flowers of a garden. Each family member comes in different colors and shapes, and each has a different personality, but our shared DNA makes an entire landscape. Some flowers are strong and can tolerate almost any soil, while others need just the right conditions to thrive. Just as gardeners know how much sun and water will grow flowers, parents help their children grow by teaching them the rules of life.

My parents didn't really know anything about bringing up children. They just had us because that's what people did in the '40s. But they didn't understand about nurturing, so my sisters and I just tried to stay out of their way. We learned through trial and error how to survive.

I have written this book to try to help others of any age endure the unfortunate things that unexpectedly happen to each of us, the nagging feelings of insecurity, and the little voice in all our heads always saying, "You'll never be good enough."

In spite of the odds coming from a family of suicide, incest, schizophrenia, manic depression, alcoholism, and cancer, I have managed to escape the parched earth of my family garden and replant myself into a healthier landscape.

Here's hoping you, too, will learn not just to survive, but to thrive in your own garden.

Part I

1

Hydrangea: Granny Elsa

My grandmother, Granny Elsa, my mother's mother, was a hydrangea, able to tolerate almost any soil, produce abundant blooms, and display many colors. In flower language, a hydrangea can symbolize either gratitude or heartlessness. Granny Elsa symbolized both. She even smelled like a hydrangea, with the odor of Cashmere Bouquet talcum powder wafting through the air wherever she walked.

During the Great Depression, when almost everyone lost their savings, my great-grandfather, who'd come to this country penniless, worked his way up to found a brokerage company. He was the first Jewish member on the New York Stock Exchange. Naturally, he brought up his children as aristocrats, expecting his daughters to marry only doctors or lawyers.

Granny Elsa obediently married a lawyer. They owned a

brownstone on New York City's Upper East Side and a country estate in Deal, New Jersey, a seaside resort for super-wealthy Jews. The Deal house had eighteen rooms with a staff addressed only as "Cook," "Nanny," "Chauffeur," "Gardener," and "Maid."

Like a hydrangea, which comes back every year, life could have continued happily ever after for my grandparents and their family. But one day, my grandfather unthinkingly helped a friend with an illegal deal. Soon after, the district attorney came knocking on the door, saying my grandfather would be arrested if he didn't get out of town. Granny Elsa was forced to divorce him to protect the family money. He fled to Chicago and died a few years later, supposedly of pneumonia, but I think it was heartbreak.

Granny Elsa (she later insisted we drop the Granny and just call her Elsa) wasted no time in finding another man. He was a doctor (of course) named Maurice Husik, but she called him "The Doctor." Elsa and the doctor appeared to be in love, but I knew he was gay. If she knew it, she never admitted it. They didn't live together, and they never married—he insisted he had to take care of his sister (who lived in a different state and whom he only saw once a year). It didn't matter. Granny Elsa was in love.

My senior year of college, I transferred from Boston University to Columbia University and moved into Elsa's posh apartment at 2 Fifth Avenue. She was eighty-four at the time and loved to recount how, back in 1952, she'd seen a building under construction and had to go up to the twenty-fifth floor on the outside construction elevator wearing a hard hat. That's when she fell in love with the two-bedroom apartment with a balcony overlooking Washington Square Park.

I'm sure she had the doctor in mind when she decorated the guest bedroom with purple-and-white toile wallpaper and matching fabric on the trundle bed. But the doctor instead chose to live a block down the street on Waverly Place. His loss was my gain, because she agreed to let me come live with her for my senior year at Columbia. The guest bedroom was now mine. I'd study at the inlaid walnut French Louis XV writing desk, and she'd come into the room and say, "Now, dearie, don't ever put anything wet on this desk without a coaster. It's very old."

"Yes, I know."

"And be careful not to knock these lamps over. They're Chinese porcelain and irreplaceable," she'd add. It was annoying to be treated like a child, but a small price to pay for a free room of my own right in the heart of Greenwich Village.

In spite of her patronizing attitude, Elsa and I did have a few good conversations. She'd tell me how she was once a suffragette and marched up Fifth Avenue clad in a white dress with a blue sash. It also wasn't as if she were just a rich old lady idling away her time. She'd graduated from Barnard College—one of its first graduates—and had been both a teacher and a social worker. In 1964, when I lived with her, she continued to volunteer three days a week, helping autistic children.

Though rich, Elsa was very thrifty because she'd lived through the Depression. She'd wheel her shopping cart to the grocery store and refuse delivery so she wouldn't have to spend an extra dollar for a tip. She'd save string and rubber bands and reuse the backs of envelopes to make lists. Each morning after breakfast, I had to fold my paper napkin because I was to use it again for dinner.

Until I lived with her, I disliked her. Like the hydrangea, she could be heartless. "You three girls will never be half as beautiful as your mother," she'd say before we were even teenagers. Then she'd compare my two sisters and me to our three male cousins of the same age.

"Why can't you girls be more like the boys?" she'd criticize. Maybe one of us had put a fork in the spoon drawer or moved the silver cigarette holder an inch from where it resided on the end table. No matter how hard we tried, we were never good enough.

The boys lived in a mansion in Scarsdale, a rich New York suburb. They lacked nothing. They even had a "playroom," a fully carpeted attic with darts and ping-pong and a chilled drink container that held unlimited Dr. Peppers. We never had a playroom, and we never lived in any one place longer than a year. We kept moving from one suburban Connecticut town to another, usually because we could no longer afford the sublet in which we were living. We spent one summer crammed into a garage in Stamford, the kind with an old-fashioned garage door and no windows.

As a result of so much moving, I ended up going to thirteen schools before I graduated from college. When people asked if I was an army brat, I'd say no, my parents were running away from life. Actually, I think they were running away from Elsa.

Much to Elsa's chagrin, my mother, a cultured Vassar graduate, chose my father, a dashing Phi Beta Kappa Brown University graduate who aspired to write crime fiction like Ellery Queen. Elsa hated my father because she didn't consider being a writer a real job, and she was convinced he would never amount to anything.

The only other person in Elsa's entire family whom she considered less than perfect was her very strange son, Bernard Jr. When we went to Elsa's for Christmas and Thanksgiving, Bernard, then in his fifties, would sit with us at the "children's table." He'd tuck his napkin under his chin and slurp his soup noisily. If my sisters or I slurped our soup, Elsa would say, "Don't slurp your soup. It's bad manners." But she never admonished Bernard for the same boorishness. One day, when I was much older, I asked Elsa what was wrong with Bernard. "He was a blue baby," she said. And that was the end of the discussion.

My mother's two sisters both married successful men. The older sister, Elizabeth, who was not in the least bit attractive, managed to snag an ambitious German immigrant, Kurt, who'd come to New York City with five dollars in his pocket and a letter of introduction to Elsa's rich father. When he saw Elizabeth, he knew she'd be his ticket to wealth. His proposal was, "I do not love you. I am only marrying you for your money." Nevertheless, she adored him. They slept in twin beds and had no children. After Elsa's father died, Kurt took over my grandfather's company. My cousins told me that someday we'd all be rich.

I wanted to know how rich, because it would affect my life. One Christmas, when I was fifteen, I asked Uncle Kurt how much

I would eventually inherit. With his grating German accent, he said as loudly as he could, "Elsa, Margie *vants* to know how much she *vill* inherit from you when you die." The room went silent.

"That's not what I said," I spat out. Everyone was staring at me. I looked at Kurt and snarled, "Don't worry. Someday you're going to die."

No one said a word. My mother shot me a mortified look. My father put his head down. Kurt looked at me with hatred, and I returned his look with a smirk. Finally, my mother's younger sister, Aunt Joan, put her arm around me. "I'm sure she didn't mean it that way," Joan said. I wished my mother or father would have said that, but neither would even look me in the eye.

Four years after that encounter, I went to live with Elsa for my senior year. We never ate dinner together because she always dined with the doctor. Her housekeeper/cook would set the table for two with the good china, and silver, and fine linen napkins. At 4:30 p.m. sharp, the housekeeper would leave, and Elsa would take her bath, dress, fasten her pearls, and come into my room to make sure her slip wasn't showing. Promptly at 5 p.m., the doctor would arrive. If he wasn't there by 5:01, Elsa would phone and say, "Husik, where are you?" She only called him Husik when she was annoyed with him. To his face, she called him Maurice.

When the doctor arrived, Elsa would remove the food from the oven, and they'd dine. After dessert, they'd adjourn to the living room and sit in the matching blue silk–upholstered armchairs to watch the news, during which, the doctor would help Elsa do arm circles for her arteriosclerosis. At 7 p.m. sharp, he'd leave. Then I'd come out from my room, reheat my dinner, and eat it on the everyday china with my paper napkin left over from breakfast.

After dinner, Elsa might engage me in a serious conversation. She'd usually begin with something like, "Margie, I don't care how successful you are in life, if you don't have love, you have nothing at all."

I'd divert the conversation. "Elsa, do you make love with the doctor?"

She'd peer at me and say, "Do I ask you if you make love with Bob?"

"Yes, I do." Bob was my first boyfriend in college, the one to whom I'd lost my virginity. I'd met him at a summer stock theater where he was the stage manager, and I was an apprentice. He was the real reason I'd transferred to Columbia, but I lied and told everyone I transferred because Columbia offered better courses.

"So, do you make love with Dr. Husik?" I'd ask again.

"Well, I *would*," she'd say, "but he has prostate problems." And that was the end of the conversation.

2

Rose: My Mother

My mother was a rose, the most beautiful flower of all. Like the rose, she had all the advantages of luxury and good breeding, and everyone envied her because her life seemed so carefree. Yet her life was anything but easy. She died almost fifty years ago. They say that once a person dies, no matter what your relationship with them, they turn into a saint. Not my mother.

I did not cry when she died at the age of seventy-five. I was relieved. I don't remember many good things about her, only the way she constantly criticized me. Nothing I did was good enough. I wanted her to leave the family and disappear. When I was eighteen, my father committed suicide. I was furious because the wrong parent had died.

My mother liked to think of herself as a Russian revolutionary because she'd once written an article for a communist newspaper,

The Daily Worker, and never stopped talking about it. She bragged about being fired from the paper because she'd criticized a film made by a communist. She told us repeatedly how, during one spring vacation at Vassar, she'd driven to West Virginia with her roommate, the poet Muriel Rukeyser, to photograph striking miners after an industrial disaster at Gauley Bridge. Muriel wrote a poem about it and my mother shot photos. In those days, she was an aspiring photographer.

While at Vassar, she studied with famous photojournalist Walker Evans. Much to my shock, a few years ago I learned that three of her photos from the mining disaster are in the Walker Evans collection at the Metropolitan Museum of Art. Perhaps she could have been a professional photographer if she hadn't had children.

Her other talent was writing, which was surprising because that's something she rarely talked about except the book she'd published, *We Make the Movies*, a book of interviews with people in the film industry. She never stopped talking about it. It turns out the book was not all she wrote. After she died, I found a suitcase in her closet full of her writings. I read a few short stories, which were good, but I was so angry with her for refusing to discuss her eventual death that I threw everything out. It is probably the stupidest thing I've ever done—or, perhaps, an act that saved me from knowing the sad truth about her unfulfilled life.

The thing that's so odd is that I, too, ended up a writer. And while my mother interviewed Hollywood people, I interview CEOs, celebs, musicians, and sports stars. Perhaps my mother and I are not so unalike after all. And while I never shot with a Leica or Hasselblad as she did, I've been told I take wonderful photographs on my iPhone. Maybe my mother would have been a success had it not been the 1940s when women didn't have careers. Or maybe it was my grandmother's fault. Granny Elsa, who was of German heritage, repeatedly told her three daughters that a woman's role should be *Kirche, Küche,* and *Kinder* (Church, Kitchen, and Children).

As far as church was concerned, both my parents were Jewish, but they didn't believe in organized religion. I think my father was rebelling from his strict Jewish upbringing, and my mother didn't seem to have any religion. Years later, as my mother lay dying in hospice, she said, "If only I had brought you children up with religion." I tried to tell her it made no difference. My religion has always been nature. As far as kitchen, when my mother was growing up, "Cook" took care of all meals. My mother could only make two meals: boiled hot dogs (with no roll), and what she called "chicken cacciatore"—broiled chicken with Campbell's Tomato Soup dumped on top. When my parents went out to dinner, we were allowed Swanson's TV dinners, a real treat. As for children, my parents always said we were to be seen and not heard. While it was never openly discussed, my father wanted a boy, and my mother gave up trying after three girls and one abortion. We were eighteen months apart, me in the middle. One day, when I was about eight, my mother turned to us and said, "Don't have children. It's not worth it." I think she resented us because it meant she could never have a career.

One day, when I was eleven, my mother had to go into the hospital for a biopsy of a lump on her breast. Children weren't allowed to visit. That afternoon, when I came home from school, my father was sitting in the living room, sobbing. I'd never seen a man cry before, certainly not my father. Instead of doing a biopsy, the surgeon determined my mother had cancer and thought it was safer to remove both breasts. He never woke her up to ask her wishes because he didn't want her to have to be re-anesthetized. My mother returned home, brutally disfigured. She bought a mastectomy bra with two heavy silicone breast forms. I could never watch her get dressed, because I didn't want to see the two huge scars slicing her now flat chest.

My sympathy for my mother didn't last long, because once she was healed, she went back to criticizing me for everything, just as her own mother had criticized her. When my mother had told Elsa she planned to marry my father, a young writer, Elsa said, "He's not good enough for you." So, my mother and father packed their belongings and drove cross-country to San Francisco, married, and had the three of us.

Later, my mother told me she only had kids because her gynecologist said everyone else was having children. My father said they had kids so he could avoid the draft. They had no idea how much it cost to feed and clothe three kids, money which they sorely lacked. My father couldn't make a living as a writer, so he took a job in the San Francisco shipyards and then as a Fuller Brush salesman. Nothing panned out. Finally, they swallowed their pride and sent a Western Union telegram to Elsa, begging for money. She said they'd have to move back to New York if they expected to see a penny. With no other choice, they piled the three of us into the back seat of the old Ford and drove east. There, they settled into a cheap rental in Bell Island, Connecticut—now an outrageously pricey town, but back then, cheap, sleepy, and close enough to NYC to accept Elsa's handouts.

I don't think of my mother as a beautiful rose because I can't get past her thorns. Starting with kindergarten, on Elsa's dime, I was sent to a private nursery school in Rowayton, Miss Thomas's School for Girls, which I loved, but in the middle of the year, my parents yanked me out and transferred me to a public school. "We don't want you growing up like one of those white-faced debutantes," my mother said. In retrospect, I'm sure they had a fight with Elsa about the money. She was already paying for our shoes and school clothes, Girl Scout camp one week each summer, and the various Connecticut house rentals. I would never again experience a private school. What I missed most about Miss Thomas's School was my teacher, who always encouraged me, saying, "You can do anything." Whereas with my mother, if I showed her something I'd done in school, such as making a wooden napkin holder, she'd say, "How come *you* can do that? I could never do that."

Everything with her was a competition. Once, I was shooting hoops in our driveway when my mother, who had never played basketball, approached with two long sticks.

"Come on," she said, "I'll teach you how to fence." The minute she showed me what to do, she hit me repeatedly with the stick, her blue eyes angry little slits.

"Stop it," I yelled. "You're hurting me." But she continued to strike, a smirk on her face, thrilled that finally she could do something better than me.

In all fairness, I am painting her as a witch. Not true, she did the best she could. I certainly wouldn't want to be stuck in the house all day with three screaming daughters. I just wish she had given me some advice.

When I was thirteen, a boy asked me out on my first date to the ice cream parlor. I didn't want to go. He was short and had a shock of red hair. My mother encouraged the date. When I finally agreed, she said, "Always let a boy be right, and always be subservient. Just be a lady." Ruth Bader Ginsburg's mother also told her to be a lady, but her mother's idea of being a lady was to be your own person. My mother's only other advice to me was, "Be happy." But what does that mean? Who's in a permanent state of happiness? I wish she'd told me, "I don't care what you do. Just be the best."

My mother was different than all the other mothers. She wore drab, shapeless shifts, and while every other mother had a bob, mine wore her long hair in a twist. And she never stopped asking questions. Endlessly.

During my entire childhood, we went on only two family vacations: one to Mystic, Connecticut, and the other to Washington, DC. While on a tour of the Pentagon, the guide pointed out the plaster mask of Al Capone's face and John Dillinger's gun. My mother asked, "Excuse me, but did Dillinger have a license to carry a gun?" I wanted to crawl into the floor.

My mother repeatedly told me that the happiest time in her life was when she was nine and played Alice in *Alice in Wonderland*. Each time she told the story, she'd crawl under the dining room table, cry, and say, "I miss my father so much." This, of course, was after many vodkas or glasses of Gallo wine. And if she wasn't crying about that, she'd cry about how horrible it was that her father was taken away when she was just eighteen and how much she loved him. I never connected the dots, but my father, too, was taken away from me when I was eighteen.

Once, I asked my mother why she hadn't become a writer or photographer or actress—another thing she aspired to be. She said she'd been studying acting and was cast in a play as an extra, but then she met my father and fell in love. She said that sharing his life and making a home was far more important than any kind of career. Maybe she truly believed that in the beginning, and besides, back then, women only had careers as nurses or secretaries.

My mother desperately needed to be appreciated. She started analyzing peoples' handwriting at cocktail parties, but she still didn't get the attention she craved, so she decided she was clairvoyant and began to "read" people. She'd say, "I see the letter S. Is there a letter S in your life?" Or "Is there a red rug in your home?" And people would get excited and say, "Yes! Yes! How did you know that?" I would cringe.

Then, just when I thought she'd lost all her petals and was no longer a rose, she shocked me. My first husband and I had returned from living in Paris and were looking for an apartment in New York City. Everything was either overpriced, or facing a brick wall, or too small. One day on the bus, my mother turned to a complete stranger and said, "Excuse me, but my daughter and her husband are looking for an apartment. They want two bedrooms and a terrace and a fireplace in the Village, and I think you know of such a place."

The woman looked at my mother as though she were completely insane and said, "How did you know that? My friend is a landlord and wants to rent out an apartment but doesn't want to put an ad in the paper because she doesn't want millions of people tramping through." And that is how my first husband and I moved into our two-bedroom Greenwich Village fifth-floor walk-up with a large terrace overlooking a playground and rent stabilized at $158.14 per month.

3

Yellow Carnation: My Father

The carnation comes in several colors: pink symbolizes gratitude, red is love, white for purity and good luck, and yellow is disappointment and rejection. That was my father, Eugene Goldsmith. His parents divorced when he was young, which he thought was because his father didn't love him. His younger brother became a successful engineer, but Gene wanted to be a writer, an occupation of which his father disapproved, though he was proud Gene had graduated Phi Beta Kappa at Brown University.

Sometime after he finished college, my father wrote two mystery novels: *Murder on His Mind* and *Layout for a Corpse*. Neither sold well enough for him to write full-time. After a few failed part-time jobs, he became an advertising copywriter. He would return from work and by his second martini would say to my mother, "This is shit. This isn't writing, it's shit."

"Nonsense," my mother would say.

He couldn't hold onto a job and was let go at four advertising agencies. When I was fifteen, we moved from Connecticut to Philadelphia because a new agency had hired him. Yet, soon after, he came home reeking of alcohol, fired again. He smiled sheepishly and said, "Last hired, first fired."

It was hurtful to see his sad brown eyes each time he returned from a potential job that he had failed to get. I loved him so much and wanted nothing more than for him to find a good job. His mother, my other grandmother, Gram, also loved him unconditionally. Gram wasn't rich, so she never dangled money the way Elsa did, but she was exceedingly generous. If my father was a disappointed yellow carnation, Gram was the red carnation of love. At Christmas, she'd give me and my sisters pillowcases full of presents.

On Thanksgiving and Christmas, we were forced to go to both grandmothers' homes. Gram and my father would hold hands under the dining room table, and my mother resented it, though I don't know why, because my mother was not a touchy-feely person. She never hugged or kissed me unless I was sick. And the only time she said she loved me was when I moved to Paris.

My father, though, was very affectionate. He was six foot three, with hands as big as baseball mitts and size thirteen feet. When we went to the beach in Rowayton, he'd hoist me on his shoulders and fling me into the water. Then he'd lie down on a towel next to my mother and I'd notice something. Like the carnation, which can be floppy because the flowers are too heavy to support the stems, part of my father's penis would hang out. I'd look away, figuring they must not make bathing trunks long enough for such a tall man.

My father seemed to have the same problem with his pajamas. His pajama fly never stayed closed. If it was early morning and my sisters and I were playing loudly in the hallway, he'd fling open the bedroom door and tell us to shut up. Each time, his penis was hanging out of his pajamas. Now, I think he might have done it on purpose.

Once, when I was about ten, he had jaundice. My mother was at her volunteer job and we were playing cards with my father, all of us sitting on the floor. His legs were splayed, and he was stark naked. I didn't know what jaundice was but figured it must be something that hurt if you were wearing clothes. The doorbell rang and there were footsteps on the stairs. As the doctor walked in, my father grabbed a pillow and held it in front of his thighs. I don't remember the excuse he gave the doctor, but I do remember the doctor looking at him very strangely.

But there were good days, when my father would put Rodgers & Hart's "Bewitched, Bothered and Bewildered" on the Victrola and I'd place my bare feet on top of his enormous brown Oxfords as he waltzed me around the room. It was wonderful to have him to myself if only for a few minutes.

Desperate to be the boy he always wanted, I took up tennis. He'd wake me up at 7 a.m. and we'd drive to the public courts and play for an hour before school. It was particularly special because neither sister played tennis, so again, I had him to myself. That was the good part. We'd come home and he'd pull off his shirt, lie on the bed, and tell me to give him a massage. As he was so big, I'd have to clamber onto his sweaty back to dig into his shoulders. I hated the smell of his dried sweat, and I couldn't stand my bare sticky legs straddled on his back. But I said nothing.

My father and mother both drank three martinis before dinner, which I figured was normal, but nothing was normal in my house. My great-aunt once said, "I pity you three girls." I had no idea what she meant. Maybe she knew my father had a violent streak. When he was angry, he'd storm into his den and slam the French door so violently I thought a pane would shatter. I'd hide, hoping he wouldn't take it out on me.

When he was angry, his face turned crimson, his lower lip quivered, and his mouth morphed into a snarl. Then, those same palms that had gripped my hands so sweetly as he flew me in the air when we played angel would whack me on the back of my head. To this day, if anyone's hand comes too close, I flinch. He never took his anger out on Kathy or Lynne. Kathy had her own problems and Lynne was the youngest.

Once, when I was wearing a skirt, he was so furious for whatever I'd done that he hung me upside down, gripped both my ankles in one huge hand, and whacked my buttocks again and again. It wasn't the hitting that hurt; it was the humiliation—he could see my white Carter's underpants. After he released his grip, I'd race to my room and cover my head with a pillow. I would never allow him to hear me cry.

Now and then, there was a full week of peace, but then something would trigger his anger such as the Fourth of July, when we drove to watch the fireworks. The year I was fifteen, I had a boyfriend and wanted to skip the fireworks, but my father wouldn't allow it. He practically dragged me into the back seat. At one point, we stopped for a red light. I pulled open the door and ran out into the street, determined to run home. My father tore open his door, chased me, caught up, grabbed my arm, and kicked my shin again and again. I hated him.

Before we moved to a Philadelphia suburb, we were living in a house in South Norwalk with one bathroom. The shower had only enough hot water for one person. I'd come home from basketball practice and need to wash my hair. My mother would tell me she planned to wash her hair, so I couldn't. But one time when my parents were having dinner (we always ate before them), I sneaked into the bathroom, locked the door, and climbed into the shower. I was rinsing my hair when suddenly there was a loud banging on the door.

"Open that door immediately, you little brat," my father screamed.

"I can't go to school with my hair dirty," I called back.

"That hot water is for your mother. Open the door now!"

Bang! He smashed his fist into the door. The hook bounced off the latch, he pulled open the shower curtain, and he dragged me out of the shower naked. "Don't you ever do that again ever. Do you understand?" he screamed.

I reached for a towel and tried to cover myself, but he was staring at my naked body. It was humiliating.

One Sunday morning, we were having breakfast at the dining room table (we always ate together on Sundays). My mother was in the kitchen and for reasons unknown, the swinging door was closed. My father beckoned me to sit on his lap. I did, and suddenly, he groped my breasts. I was appalled but afraid to say anything. Kathy and Lynne both looked horrified but neither dared say a word. As he touched me, he said quietly, "Ooh, look at all the milk we could get out of those."

I couldn't tell my mother because of her double mastectomy. Years later, I told a shrink, who insisted my mother had to have known and purposely closed the door. I don't think so.

When I was eighteen, a freshman at Boston University, I was summoned to the housemother's office and, out of nowhere, was told my father was dead. He had committed suicide, jumping from the fourteenth story of the building where he was working in downtown Philadelphia. In the 1960s, suicide was something that was never said out loud. When my friends called, I told them he'd fallen out of a window by mistake.

I tried to picture the scene. It was a Saturday, so no one would have been at the advertising agency. He'd lied to my mother about having to work that day. Did he lock his office door first? Did he take a drink from his dented silver flask?

He left a typed letter on yellow copy paper saying he loved us, he knew that my mother, Lynne, and I would be fine, and he only wished he could take Kathy with him. It was less than a month before Christmas. He had to have opened the office window. Did he climb right out on the ledge or did he hesitate? What was he thinking the instant he stepped into the air? The police returned his possessions: a wallet with two crumpled dollar bills, a shattered pair of eyeglasses, and a wristwatch with a broken crystal.

My mother told me he'd tried to commit suicide twice before, once when Kathy was born, and once while at college. I learned he'd had shock treatment in the past and was due to go into the hospital the day he killed himself, but he hated the procedure and told my mother to cancel the bed. For months afterward, my mother lay sobbing on the living room sofa drinking herself into a vodka oblivion repeating, "If only I hadn't cancelled the bed."

The day before he killed himself, my father had taken Kathy to her first locked mental institution, Eastern Pennsylvania Psychiatric Institute. He told my mother that as he said goodbye and the thick steel door locked behind him, he felt as though he were the one who should have been inside. The night of his death, I couldn't sleep, so I went into his den and rummaged through the desk drawer. Hidden under some papers was a small black notebook with his familiar scrawl:

Wednesday: Bad. Friday: Worse. Tuesday: Terrible.

If someone asks how your father died and you say heart attack or cancer, they tell you how sorry they are, and the subject is over. But if you say "suicide," they look shocked and say, "Suicide?" This is not a substitute for "I'm sorry," but rather a shortcut to what they really want to know: Did he take pills? Slit his wrists? Shoot himself? I usually tell people my father died in a freak accident, and they let it go. Forty-eight years after his death on 9/11, the Twin Towers fell. The news showed people jumping from buildings—people who wanted to live, but died. My father had chosen the opposite.

My family was dysfunctional before he did it, but afterward, we were wounded in new ways. My mother blamed herself. Kathy spent the rest of her life in mental institutions and halfway houses. Lynne never said much, but I knew how hurt she was. I handled it by drinking myself into oblivion, doing drugs, and spending years in therapy.

And though it happened over sixty years ago, there are still moments when I visualize his body hurtling toward the ground and wonder, in those last few moments, if only for a brief second, did he think of me?

4

Goutweed: My Older Sister

Goutweed is an invasive ground cover that is never satisfied and pushes other plants aside, making life difficult for those around it. That was my older sister, Kathy. As a toddler, Kathy was the beautiful child with a sweet smile, blue eyes, and long, golden-blond hair. When Kathy was three, she took her toy scissors and snipped off every tulip in our neighbor's garden, but my parents didn't punish her because their bible was Dr. Spock's book, *Baby and Child Care*. For my parents, the letter P did not stand for Punishment—it stood for Permissive, the way Dr. Spock taught parents to bring up their children.

Kathy acted out constantly, and my parents were unable to control her. Once, Granny Elsa was so frustrated with her tantrums that she threw a wooden spoon, which hit Kathy in the eye. They rushed Kathy to the hospital, but fortunately, nothing was wrong. My other grandmother, Gram, never threw anything at Kathy, but when Kathy was three, Gram said, "Something's wrong with that child. I can see it in her eyes."

Kathy would scream at the top of her lungs whenever she didn't get her way. My father never hit her, but she was constantly docked her allowance—fifty cents a week—and Kathy didn't care. One day, fed up with all the yelling and with no one paying any attention to me, I decided to run away. I packed my Girl Scout mess kit and Sterno camping stove, grabbed some bread and eggs, left a note, and ran about a quarter of a mile down the road to a dense thicket. I fried the eggs, ate, and wondered what to do next. After about an hour, I walked home and tore up the note. No one knew I'd been missing.

When Kathy was seven, they sent her to a child psychiatrist, but Kathy continued to rage. Once, she was screaming so loudly, the neighbors called the police. My father told them we were just rehearsing a play. They believed it. Kathy got worse. At school, I told everyone I wasn't her sister. If she had a friend over and I wanted to play with them, she'd slam her bedroom door and scream, "Play with your own friends, bucktooth." It was so hurtful.

Kathy began to knock on doors in the neighborhood, saying she was an orphan and asking them to adopt her. Often, the police brought her home. She didn't care when my parents punished her; our home was in constant turmoil. Once, I wrote an essay about Kathy for English class. The teacher ripped it up and said I should stop making up stories.

Because it was the 1950s, no one talked about mental illness. My parents sent Kathy to different psychiatrists, but nothing worked. Her tantrums got worse. They had no idea what to do. We kept moving to new neighborhoods, not because of her, but mainly because they wanted to find a place cheap enough not to have to take Granny Elsa's handouts. Kathy acted out just as much no matter where we lived. For me, that meant yet another new school and having to make new friends all over again. By the time I graduated from college, I had gone to thirteen different schools.

Kathy got worse. Finally, they sent her to a school for emotionally disturbed teens, Moravian Seminary, outside of Philadelphia. We said she was at boarding school. But Moravian Seminary couldn't control her, either. She was transferred to a new psychiatric boarding school and classified as a schizophrenic. I was sure this was all my parents' fault because all her life, they'd let her get away with murder. I hoped she'd get back to normal, come home, and we'd be friends at last. The day I got my driver's license, I went to visit her. The girls there were very strange, and I was sure they were making her worse. I left disappointed and angry.

Eventually, Kathy was so disruptive, she was asked to leave the school. They sent her to a psychiatric institute where you needed to be buzzed in through two locked doors to enter. I couldn't believe she was locked up. My father couldn't either. The day after he visited her was the day he ended his life. My mother didn't tell Kathy he had died because none of us wanted her at the funeral. She'd be too disruptive. Three months later, my mother told her. A couple of months after that, Kathy was sent to Tri-County, a home in Quakertown, Pennsylvania, for people with developmental disabilities. They called it a halfway house because it was halfway between a supervised adult rooming house and an unlocked psychiatric facility. Lynne and I would drive two hours from New York City to visit her every year at Christmas and on her birthday.

When my mother died, I became Kathy's trustee, looking over the small inheritance from both parents' deaths. This made visits to her even more depressing because Kathy was obsessed with money. When Lynne and I arrived at Tri-County, we'd walk through the living room where the other patients sat staring vacantly into space. The moment we entered her room, Kathy would say, "Margie, I need money, please? Can I have some money?" I'd look at her face, now lined with wrinkles, and her thinning, prematurely gray hair held back by a childish red headband. Her lips smacked together because of tardive dyskinesia, a side effect of her antipsychotic drugs. "Please, Margie?" Her allowance was ample. I'd always say no.

Then she'd say, "Mr. Weatherill is in the closet, trying to steal my money."

Mr. Weatherill was the father of her boyfriend, who'd been transferred to a different psychiatric hospital. Since then, Kathy had been obsessed with his father, whom she claimed lived in her closet. "He's in there, and the social worker is hiding my money. I want more money." She'd fold her arms across her chest.

"We'll discuss it later," I'd say, trying not to lose my temper, but Kathy's constant demands would drive me into a rage. I understood her panic. For years, I also thought I'd be penniless because we were brought up with so little. Then I'd say, "Mr. Weatherill is in your closet?" I'd pull open the closet door. On the floor were at least twenty-four pairs of red shoes with flat heels. "Kathy, why all the red shoes?"

"I like them."

Behind the shoes were a dozen dirty coffee cups and saucers. "What's this?" I'd ask.

"That's for Mr. Weatherill."

One day, a miracle happened. Doug Eshbach, a social worker, joined Tri-County's staff. He loved Kathy and, because he had a car, we no longer had to drive to Quakertown. Each Christmas, Doug would drive with Kathy to Manhattan. We'd see a matinee of the *Nutcracker*, have a steak dinner, and then Doug would drive her back home. The same thing on her birthday. During one of her birthday visits, we were in a restaurant eating dinner when Kathy turned to me and said, "Can I have a mink coat? Please, Margie? I want a mink coat." Her mouth was full of half-chewed steak.

"Kathy, please don't talk with your mouth full," I said. Lynne shot me a "can't-you-shut-her-up?" look.

Lynne didn't understand that Kathy wasn't doing this on purpose. The cloth napkin tucked into the collar of Kathy's dress began to slip, and Doug tenderly tucked it back in.

Fifteen years later, Doug and Kathy were still coming to New York City. Kathy was now fifty-five but seemed much older. The many drugs she took did that—Lithium, Clozaril, Risperdal, and

Zyprexa. I didn't even know what they gave her, but the drugs made her hands shake, and sometimes she'd slur her words so badly I couldn't understand a word. Her face was even more wrinkled, and her hair was thinner, still held back by a red hairband. Her clothes hung from her body because she'd lost at least twenty pounds. "I'm going to the bathroom," she'd say. I'd watch her walk away, then she'd turn, wave, and smile like a sweet child. It broke my heart because she looked so helpless. Almost immediately, she'd return to the table.

"That was fast," I'd say.

"I didn't have to go." She'd plop down in her chair, take a huge bite of steak, and smile at me, her mouth full of food. "I love you, Margie," she'd say.

I had to stop myself from tearing up.

At 9 p.m. on New Year's Eve, going into the year 2000, the manager of Tri-County called to say that Kathy had died of a heart attack. I didn't believe him because Kathy had never had heart trouble. I demanded an autopsy. Later, I learned that Kathy had gone to the main house, saying she was feeling sick. They'd called the doctor. Kathy said she was hungry, so they gave her a roast beef sandwich and told her to go lie down in one of the bedrooms off the kitchen. I don't know if they ever came to check up on her, but the autopsy report said she'd choked to death on a sandwich.

Lynne and I drove to Quakertown for the last time. The residents had arranged a small memorial service, and various people said nice words about Kathy. After, we went to her room to see if there was anything worth taking. The drawers were crammed with at least twenty brand-new wool sweaters from Talbots whose tags hadn't even been removed. The red shoes and empty coffee cups and saucers were at the bottom of the closet. We took nothing.

I thought about Kathy's sad life, the highlight of which had been going to the mall once a week to play bingo. I wish I'd been able to help her, but there was nothing I could do. It must have been awful to be all alone and choking. I just hope she didn't suffer too much.

5

Lipstick Plant: My Younger Sister

Just before it opens and blooms, the lipstick plant looks like a beautiful red tube of lipstick. Too little sun and it won't bloom; too much water and the roots rot. The lipstick plant needs just the right amount of attention to thrive, like my younger sister, Lynne, who thrived in spite of too little nurturing, a testament to her survival skills.

I was always jealous of Lynne because Kathy, eighteen months older than me, received constant attention by being disruptive. Lynne, eighteen months younger, got attention because she was adorable and helpless. My father never hit her or touched her inappropriately. Lynne and I fought constantly, even over who would wear which black hat for my father's funeral. A year after my father died, my mother moved from Philadelphia to New York, where Lynne and I shared the second bedroom. Because we were both in college, we only saw each other during school vacations.

Soon after I graduated college, I went to Paris on a two-hundred-dollar Columbia University charter flight and decided to stay. It was in 1965, the days when long distance cost a fortune and cell phones, Skype, and Zoom had not yet been invented. It was too expensive for my mother to call, so finally, I could escape her constant criticism and disappointment that I was not yet married. I was free.

One day, after living in Paris only six months, Lynne showed up unannounced. I was living with John, an American expat film director who would become my first husband. John and I had just moved in together, so Lynne's timing could not have been worse, and I told her she couldn't stay. Kicking her out was the cruelest thing I ever did to her, and it haunts me to this day.

Four years later, after I moved back to NYC, I divorced husband number one, and Lynne and I developed a semi-amiable relationship because by then, we were both divorced and lonely. A few weekends, we'd take the bus together to a yoga retreat near Woodstock, New York, sipping the entire way from a gallon jug of Gallo wine. Once there, we'd smoke pot and spend the weekend doing yoga. About ten years later, she met Howard and has been with him ever since. By then, I'd met husband number two, so except for when we visited Kathy, we didn't see much of each other.

It is now forty years later, and we finally understand and appreciate each other. We are the last two living members of the entire family. Often, we'll share our memories. She'll say, "Do you remember when we lived in Jenkintown and Daddy was mowing the lawn and he mowed everything except that big rectangular patch in the middle?"

"No." I had no recollection.

"How can you not remember that?" she'd ask. "He mowed everything except the very center, where he left this unmowed area the size of a casket and said, 'That's for my coffin.'"

I'd offer, "Remember the anchovies?"

"What anchovies?" she'd ask.

"He took the three of us shopping at the A&P, and when we went to leave, the manager stopped him and said, 'Don't you have something in your pocket you want to return?' Daddy turned crimson and said, 'Who, me? I have nothing.' And the manager said, 'If you don't take that out of your pocket now, I'm going to have to call the police.'"

My father's eyes looked mournful as he said, "Please, have a heart. Not in front of my daughters." He took the anchovies out of his pocket, handed them to the manager, and said, "They must have fallen into my pocket."

The manager said, "If this ever happens again, I'll have you arrested."

Eventually, we ran out of "do-you-remembers," because sometimes memories are so painful it's easier to bury them than dredge up the past. The important thing is that ten years ago, we finally stopped fighting and became friends. I was about to have a Whipple procedure to remove a cancerous tumor in the head of my pancreas, an operation from which people sometimes die. Lynne and Howard not only took me to the hospital and were waiting when I was brought up to my room, but she came to visit every day, even though she hates hospitals.

Two years later, I had stage four pancreatic cancer, and they removed my entire pancreas. Lynne visited every day. Two years after that, I developed lung cancer, and they took out my lower right lobe. She was there. A year after that, I woke up in a bed full of blood, an ulcer bleed. My blood pressure was sixty over forty, and I almost bled out before the ambulance arrived. Lynne was waiting for me in the ER. I have had nineteen hospital visits since 2014, and Lynne has been there for me every time. And ever since the Whipple, she calls each night just to make sure I'm still breathing. If that isn't love, I don't know what is.

6

Cobra Lily: Me, the Early Years

In my garden, I am the cobra lily, a plant whose dramatic leaves resemble the heads of cobras preparing to strike. This carnivorous plant grows in boggy areas devoid of nutrition, just like the one in which my parents raised me. Fortunately, I got myself out of the bog, because I share that inner strength that protects us even if we're stuck in a quagmire. For me, it came in the form of getting away fast.

We weren't allowed to leave the dinner table until we'd finished everything on our plates. "Think of the starving children in China," my mother repeated constantly. I scarfed down every meal so I could race out before my father came home. Most days, I'd tell my mother something like "Go to hell" for one thing or another. As she had no control over me, she'd say, "Wait till your father comes home. You will be severely punished." There was no telling what he might do, so I'd eat fast and run to the school playground. One time, he drove to the playground, slapped me hard in front of all my friends, and dragged me back home.

Humiliation was my middle name. When my parents didn't want to take money from Granny Elsa, my mother would drag us to the thrift store for school clothes. Going into the third grade (my fifth school since nursery school), my mother took us to buy shoes. I wanted loafers, but she insisted on "sensible" shoes, in this case, ugly brown oxfords. I argued, but to no avail. "I don't want you to ruin your feet the way I did," she said.

The first day of class, a girl next to me pointed at the dreaded shoes and snickered. Soon, the entire class was laughing. I tried to hide my feet under the desk. At recess, teams were picked for kickball. No one knew me, so no one chose me. I held back my tears. Finally, the gym teacher chose a team for me. When it was my turn, I kicked the ball farther than anyone, and suddenly I was no longer the most unpopular girl in my class. Later, I played tennis and basketball, all of which saved me because no matter how many times we moved, I made new friends through sports.

We moved so much that there wasn't always a friend around when I needed one. Writing saved me. By the time I was eight, I had written and illustrated stories, all about children who ran away from home. Once, I sent a letter to the famous author Ludwig Bemelmans, who had written the Madeline books about twelve little girls living at a boarding school in Paris. I was afraid to ask him to adopt me, so instead I asked him to draw me a picture of Silly Willy, a seal who lived in a bathtub, which I'd seen in a comic strip. Bemelmans sent back a letter with an ink drawing of Silly Willy. It said, "Dear Margie, I think Silly Willy looked something like this." Seventy years later, the letter hangs in my bathroom, a reminder that in spite of everything, there is some kindness in the world.

I left home one week each summer, when Elsa paid to send us to Girl Scout camp. I was happy, free of fights, fists, and constant criticism. I slept in a tent, walked through the woods breathing in the intoxicating scent of pine trees, and was lulled to sleep by the sound of raindrops hitting the canvas tent roof. All the other campers had arrived not knowing anyone, so I pretended not to be afraid. I'd go to each tent, smile, and introduce myself, which always got me elected unit captain, as I was the only one whose name everyone knew. Pretending and smiling became my coping mechanism.

My life was not completely *Running with Scissors*. When my father wasn't drunk or in a rage, he was funny and clever, and I adored him. It was rare that I felt any warmth from my mother; she never hugged me, never kissed me (except when I was sick), and never told me she loved me. Plus, she constantly interfered in my life, such as the day she made an unannounced appearance to my eighth-grade classroom. She waved my last assignment at my teacher and said, "Why are you giving her an A? There are three misspelled words. That doesn't deserve an A in my book." The teacher explained that the exercise was about footnotes, and I'd been the only one to get them all correct. "It's the principle," my mother argued. "You can't give someone an A if they misspell three words. How do you expect her to learn how to spell?"

At least she didn't make an appearance when I was in another new school for ninth grade. I hung out with my friends on the girls' basketball team. I had my first real boyfriend, who smelled like Old Spice. My friends threw me a surprise birthday party, my first ever, and for the first time, I was truly happy. Then my father, who had been out of work for three months, said he'd found a new job at an advertising agency in Philadelphia. We'd be moving from Connecticut, and I'd start tenth grade at Abington High School, a suburb of Philly. It was the worst news of my life.

7

My High School Years

I hated the new move from Connecticut to Philadelphia. Worse, at Abington High School, everyone had been classmates since first grade, and they didn't need new friends. I figured I'd fit in by playing sports, but there was no basketball till winter and no tennis till spring. The fall sport for girls was field hockey, a game I'd never played before. There was no writers' group, so I joined the poetry club, whose members were very snobby. The teacher read my poem out loud and asked, "Who do you think wrote this?"

"Emily Dickinson?" someone said.

"Robert Frost," guessed another.

"No. It was Margie." The class seemed shocked, then angry. None offered to have me join them for lunch. They totally ignored me, so I quit.

I was miserable until the school election was announced. One of the girls in my homeroom, Sherry Clinchard, was running for treasurer. She was a champion swimmer, popular, and had a fraternal twin sister, Enid, who was equally popular and also a great athlete. They were the kinds of friends I longed for, but to them, I was invisible. So, I came up with a plan. I introduced myself to Sherry and asked if I could be her campaign manager. She was thrilled.

Maybe my handmade posters and stickers led to her victory, but she would have won anyway. Soon, I was hanging out with Sherry, Enid, and their close friends. Finally, I was part of a group. There was just one problem—they all played field hockey, and I had no idea how to play. For away games, they piled onto the school bus, and I was left out. Then, I joined the school newspaper, which didn't cover girls' sports, so I created my own column. Not only could I ride the bus with my friends, but I also got my first byline.

I thought my parents would be proud, but either they were too drunk to care or didn't think it was a big deal. Maybe they were just busy dealing with Kathy, who'd been kicked out of school and was now in a halfway house. My grandmother, my father's mother, cared. She sent a letter heaping me with praise and enclosing a five-dollar bill, a huge amount of money back then. In my thank-you letter, I asked if she could help me get a summer job as an apprentice at *The New York Times*. She said she'd try and help. Nothing happened. Later, when she died, my great-aunt sent back all my letters, including one my grandmother had sent to my parents: "Margie wants me to help her get a job at *The New York Times*. Who does she think she is?"

At least I had my new friends. We took turns having sleepovers at each other's homes and I was terrified to be host because my parents would be drunk and embarrass me. One time, though, all my friends came over to surprise me.

We were all fifteen years old, but my mother offered us beer. Everyone thought she was the coolest. No one noticed she was drunk. The same wasn't true about my father. One night, he was supposed to pick up me and my friends from the movies, but he didn't show, so we watched the feature a second time. Finally, he staggered down the aisle and tapped me on the shoulder. He reeked of alcohol. How he drove us all home without killing anyone is a miracle. Many years later, I found out he wanted to kill the whole family and himself by driving off a cliff.

By early spring of senior year, all my friends had been accepted to college. I was sure I'd get into Sarah Lawrence because Muriel Rukeyser, my mother's former Vassar roommate, was teaching there. I was rejected. Maybe because during my interview, I asked if they had basketball and tennis teams, and when I learned they did not, I couldn't stop the tears. I told the admissions officer there was something in my eye, but I think crying was the dealbreaker. I applied to Boston University in June and, thankfully, I got in.

The summer before I left for college, I was accepted as an apprentice at Bucks County Playhouse in New Hope, Pennsylvania. By now, I wanted to be a playwright and figured hanging around theatres would help. My mother had other plans. "You will *not* spend a summer doing something useless," she said. "You will apply to Eastern Psychiatric Institute and work with the disturbed children." I pleaded with her, but she'd already arranged an interview for me at the institute.

When I walked through the locked front door, it reminded me of visiting Kathy. An employee took me to the children's playroom. A small boy came up and, as I said hello, he kicked me hard. A little girl stood in a corner picking her nose. Another boy ran up and hit me in the stomach. I would *never* work with these children.

Driving home from the interview, a taxi went through a red light and broadsided me. Blood poured out of my head and knee. The driver behind helped me into his car and rushed me to the hospital. An hour later, my head and knee had been stitched up, but I couldn't walk without crutches. My parents arrived. As we drove back home, I said I would never work at the institute. They finally agreed to let me work in summer stock but warned me not to get friendly with the hippies.

At Bucks County Playhouse, I learned to build sets, place props, use a mat knife and gaffer tape, and help some actors into their costumes. I'd never been more excited in my life, and it was over much too soon. My father drove me to Boston University, where my roommate, Gaye Todd from Fredericksburg, Virginia, became my best friend. She was the first African American I'd ever really known, and we were inseparable. When her father visited, they invited me to join them for dinner, my first meal outside of the cafeteria. There was so much love and affection between the two of them that I had to hold back my tears. Later, after a stellar career as a teacher (and Virginia's teacher of the year), she became Gaye Todd Adegbalola, an award-winning blues singer, guitarist, and songwriter, fronting a group called Saffire—The Uppity Blues Women. I had no idea until when sixty years later, she saw my byline in an article I'd written, and we reconnected.

Freshman year of college, a few weeks before Christmas vacation, a friend of my parents showed up at my dorm and escorted me into the housemother's living room. "You have to go home," she said. "Your father is very sick."

"Don't be ridiculous," I said. "My father never gets sick."

"I'll help you pack your things."

"What's the matter with him?"

"He's . . . had an accident."

"What kind of accident?"

"Your father . . ."

"What? Tell me! *What?*"

"He's dead," she said. She clutched her purse so hard her knuckles turned white. She had to be lying. Not my father. Not dead. I gasped for air. The yellow flower–patterned wallpaper in the room spun.

"I don't believe you." I struggled for air.

"He . . . jumped out of a window."

"He would *never* do that," I screamed.

The woman handed me a pill. "Take it. It's Valium. It will calm you down." She handed me a tiny envelope. "There's another one in here. Save it for later. It will help you sleep." She put her hand on my shoulder. "Let's go up to your room and pack, and then I'll drive you to the airport. You can take the shuttle."

I don't know how I made it onto the shuttle. The plane taxied down the runway and climbed into the darkening sky. How could he have left us like that? Why couldn't it have been my mother instead?

8

Bob, My First Boyfriend

I returned to Boston University after the worst Christmas of my life, trying to hide my sadness. There was no boyfriend to comfort me. In high school, I had briefly dated a good-looking football player who wasn't terribly smart. The better looking the guy, the more I thought people respected me. A few months after Christmas, I went to a mixer at Sigma Alpha Epsilon, known for their partying. I was a very good dancer—we all did the Twist back then, and the music was nonstop. I was twisting with a guy, and the entire room circled around us, hollering their encouragement. I ate up the attention. Gordy, with whom I was dancing, asked me out. Like me, he'd moved around all his life and had gone to nine different schools before BU. We had so much in common. We were both from nowhere.

"Were you an army brat too?" he asked.

"No." I didn't want to tell him we moved because my father kept getting fired. "I think my parents were running away from life," I laughed. One night, we went back to his room, and he put a tie on the doorknob, a sign to his frat brothers to keep out. Soon our clothes were off.

"Come on, baby. I'll just go in a little. Please!"

"No, I'm a virgin and I'm staying one." I could almost hear my mother's voice saying, "Don't give it away, because once a man takes your virginity, he'll have what he wants, and he'll never marry you." I got dressed, and when he took me home, he said he'd take me skiing the next weekend at Jiminy Peak. I'd never skied, and here was this handsome guy asking me to come with him.

"I don't have skis," I said.

"Don't worry, we'll rent them."

He'd said *we*. That had to mean he was paying. "So, what do I need to ski in?'

"A parka and ski pants."

I'd just gotten my one-hundred-dollar allowance for the month: twenty-five a week for lunch, the MTA, and whatever other expenses I had. I could ride my bike instead of taking the MTA, and I'd stash food from the cafeteria for lunch.

The saleslady at Filene's basement called the parka an "Anorak." I chose sage green, then tried stretchy ski pants that clung to my legs like jodhpurs. If my mother knew I was spending a hundred dollars on ski pants and a parka, she'd go crazy. But she didn't have to know.

That Saturday morning, I waited in the dorm for Gordy. My brand-new outfit was packed into my roommate's Samsonite overnight case. An hour went by—still no Gordy. He probably had a flat tire. Girls came in and out all morning, and I snapped open the suitcase to show them my new outfit. But no Gordy. Four hours later, I went upstairs, hung the new clothes in the closet, returned the suitcase, and cried. When Gaye returned, we went to see *Lawrence of Arabia*, and I kept crying, nonstop. Three days later, Gordy phoned with some lame excuse about how he had to get his car's carburetor fixed. He had an excuse for everything, and I stupidly believed it all.

I hated freshman and sophomore year, but that summer, I was accepted as an assistant property mistress at Philadelphia's Playhouse in the Park. On tech night, Doris, the prop mistress, was away, and I was waiting for notes from Bob, the stage manager. He was tall and muscular, with curly brown hair. He sat down next to me, smelling like pipe tobacco mixed with English Leather cologne. He brought his pipe to his large, Cupid-y lips. "That's all I have for props," he said, closing his notebook. "Oh, one more thing. Please tell Doris the liquid in the scotch glass for Act 1 is too dark."

I wondered if he knew how stupid Doris was. I'd told her twice the scotch didn't look real, but she just smirked and said, "What would you know? You're barely old enough to drink in a bar." I wanted Bob to know it wasn't my fault.

"Doris is a complete asshole," I said. His eyebrows shot up. "I mean, I'm sorry, I hope she's not your best friend," I mumbled.

He smiled. "She's not my best friend. Hey," he said, "would you like to have a drink after the tech tonight?"

"I'd love to." My voice sounded about three octaves higher than usual.

We sat at a small table with a red-checkered tablecloth in an Italian restaurant not far from the theatre. In the center of the table, a candle in an empty Chianti bottle dripped colored wax. The waitress came to the table. "What'll it be?" she asked.

"Two Manhattans, extra cherries," Bob said. I had no idea what a Manhattan was. I pulled out a Marlboro cigarette, and he struck a match with his fingertips. I leaned my face closer to the flickering match and inhaled the woodsy odor of his cologne. I thought about blowing a smoke ring, but wasn't sure if that would make me look sophisticated or just dumb. The Manhattans had three cherries each. "Here's to a fruitful summer," he grinned, clinking my glass. The brownish liquid burned as it slid down my throat. I was afraid I'd gag, so I swallowed a cherry.

By our third Manhattan, I learned Bob had made Phi Beta Kappa at DePauw in Indiana and had then gone to a Jesuit school to study for the priesthood. He decided against being a priest, so he got his MA and moved to New York to stage-manage off-Broadway shows at the Cherry Lane Theatre. He was presently working on his PhD thesis at Columbia. I told him I'd be a junior at Boston University in the fall, was majoring in English lit, and wanted to be a playwright.

"Oh, so that's why you're here?" He raised an eyebrow.

"Yeah, I figured it's good to be backstage to see how a play actually works."

By the time we left the restaurant, I was slightly swaying and glad I hadn't taken my car. He pulled into the parking lot of the apartment complex where we both lived, along with the rest of the theatre staff. I got out of the car and stood there, waiting for him to kiss me, but he didn't. Maybe he thought I was too young—there were eleven years between us.

"Well, thanks," I said, trying not to slur my words.

"Thank *you*," he said. "I'll walk you to your room." My room was almost directly downstairs from his.

At my door, I tried to hide my disappointment. Suddenly, he swept me into his arms and kissed me. I could taste the bourbon. He pressed his body against mine and I pulled away because there was no way I was going to sleep with him on the first date.

"Goodnight and thanks again," I said, trying to open the door before I lost my resolve. "I'll see you in the morning."

The next night, during a performance, walking by his booth, I slowed down and smiled. He looked so scholarly with his pipe. When he saw me, he winked. The next time I passed, he signaled me over, took the pipe out of his mouth, and handed me a folded note. "This is for you."

"Thanks." I took the note, walked away, unfolded the paper, and read:

"Love looks not with the eyes but with the mind." (A Midsummer Night's Dream). You look so beautiful tonight. It makes me want to leave the booth and sweep you into my arms.

I danced down the aisle to take a prop away. Should I write him back? What would I say? Two scenes later, I passed by his booth and he handed me another folded note.

"Frailty, thy name is woman!" (Hamlet, Act 1, scene 2). How about having dinner with me after the show tonight?

We sat in a restaurant, the aroma of steak wafting in the air. "Mmm, that smells good," I said.

"Why don't you have a steak?"

We never had steak at home. A waitress placed two plates of sizzling steak in front of the couple nearby. I would *love* to order a steak, but it was the most expensive thing on the menu—ten dollars. The few times we went out, my parents only allowed us to order the cheapest food.

"How do you like your steak?" Bob asked.

"Medium rare."

He ordered a bottle of Chianti, and after the waitress poured, he held up his wine glass and said, "'Love does not consist in gazing at each other, but in looking outward together in the same direction.' Do you know who said that?" It didn't sound familiar. "Antoine de Saint-Exupery," he said.

I was in love. We polished off the wine and sipped Sambuca, which I'd never even heard of, and which he'd also ordered for me without asking. I'd never felt this taken care of. "Do you know why there are three coffee beans in the Sambuca?" he asked. I shook my head. "It was a sign of the European Underground; they ordered it when they were trying to warn the US and British military not to speak because German undercover agents were around." His hand was resting on the table. I touched his palm with my own, causing the little blond hairs on my arm to stand straight up. He turned his hand over and squeezed mine. "If they put in a fourth bean, that meant get out of there fast." My head was spinning.

We stood in front of the door to my room. He kissed me and pulled me toward him. "Why don't you come upstairs to my room for a nightcap?" he said. I followed him up the outdoor staircase. His room was stacked with books, mainly plays from Aeschylus and Euripides to O'Neill and Albee. There was no comfortable place to sit, but that didn't matter because he pulled me onto the bed, and we lay there locked together. "Shall we take our clothes off, my darling?"

Oh my God. He's calling me "my darling." I could barely speak. I lifted my arms. It didn't really matter that I was wearing my Playtex support bra with the wide straps instead of my Vanity Fair lacy bra since he snapped it open expertly with one hand. "I just want to make you happy," he said.

For the rest of the summer, I couldn't wait till the performance ended each night to go back to Bob's room. On the last night. we lay on his bed. "I can't believe I have to go back to school so soon," I said.

"Well, you certainly made my summer, my darling." He took my hand and squeezed it.

"I don't want to leave you." I snuggled into him, breathing in his English Leathery scent. *Ask me to marry you when I graduate.*

He reached for his pipe and squeezed some tobacco from a pouch. "But you'll come visit me in New York," he said.

"I will?" I sat up.

"Of course," he said.

The first time I went to New York City to visit him for the weekend, I made the taxi wait until he opened the door. His apartment was in a tenement building in a seedy neighborhood on Avenue A, a railroad flat with wall-to-wall sagging bookshelves. A ladder led to a sleeping loft, where we'd spend most of the weekend. Eventually, he told me where his keys were hidden (on top of the door lintel), and I'd arrive at his apartment before he got home from the theatre. There was always a note waiting, such as, "You are such a curious blend of intelligence and sophistication—just wait till I get home."

By the end of junior year, I knew this was love, and Bob was my destiny. I transferred to Columbia University and told everyone I was transferring because I was going to write the most brilliant medieval symbolism dictionary known to mankind, but that was just to impress people. It was really about Bob. I moved in with my grandmother on lower Fifth Avenue and landed a summer job working backstage for Joe Papp at the New York Shakespeare Festival. As an assistant stage manager, I was paid twenty-five dollars for the entire summer. One day, I approached Joe and told him I had to take care of my older sister, so I needed a raise. It wasn't true, but I had no idea how to ask for more money. He glared at me and said, "Don't you ever ask for a raise using a personal reason as an excuse." I never forgot that.

Near the end of my senior year, my mother moved from Philadelphia into a two-bedroom apartment in Greenwich Village. Kathy was in the halfway house in Pennsylvania, and Lynne was a sophomore at Syracuse, so I moved into my mother's apartment. I would have moved in with Bob, but he didn't ask. Then, a week before graduation, Bob and I were at his apartment in bed. When he turned over, I saw his back was scratched with what looked like fingernail marks. My heart sank. "Bob, your back is scratched."

"Oh, I must have scraped it against the bathroom shelf."

There was no proof those were fingernail marks, so I let it go. But the next night, when I arrived at his apartment before him, I opened the drawer of his rolltop desk and flipped through a pile of papers. A pink envelope was wedged in between *Mother Courage* and *The Complete Works of Shakespeare*. There was no return address, just a red-smudged imprint of lips. I pulled the letter out of the envelope and read:

April 8, 1965
Dear Big Darling,
I'm so anxious to get back to your bed.
Love, xoxo,
Suzanne

WHAT? Who was this?

I heard his footsteps outside and shoved the note back into the envelope. He entered. I wouldn't look him in the eye.

"Hey! Happy to see me?" He grabbed my hand.

"Don't touch me."

He took the pipe out of his mouth. "What's the huff about?" He lifted up my chin with his finger, then ran his hand over my face.

"We're finished." I bit my lip to hold back the tears.

"Why, my darling?"

"You know why." Tears splashed down my cheeks.

"I don't know why at all." He put his hands on my shoulders. "What's the matter?"

How could I tell him and still keep him? Nobody had ever loved me the way he did, and if I left him, who would I go out with? I'd be alone all summer and would have to spend every night at the Quad Cinema watching foreign films, then go home to my mother for the same discussion we had nightly, which was that I needed to find a man and settle down because I was almost twenty-one. Bob was too poor, and thirty-two was much too old. If she wasn't lecturing me, she'd be three sheets to the wind, crawling under the table after her fourth glass of Gallo, rehashing the same old stories. That's what I had to look forward to.

Bob tried to caress my neck. I pulled back and said, "I thought you loved me?"

"And what makes you think I don't?" He moved toward me.

"I read a letter of yours tonight."

He laughed. "Is that so terrible?"

"Who's Suzanne?"

His eyes got wider. "Suzanne?"

"Don't pretend you don't know. You slept with her, didn't you?"

He laughed and shrugged.

"DIDN'T YOU?"

"Yes." He looked away.

"And you can admit it, just like that?"

He was silent. I was still hoping the whole thing would go away.

I decided to threaten him. This way, he'd get rid of Suzanne. That morning in front of Butler Hall, someone had been passing out flyers: *$200, Student Rate. Round-trip summer charter flight to Paris, May 5–August 24.*

"Hey," he said, moving closer, "I can make love to others in your absence, and that doesn't in the least diminish my love for you." Was I hearing him correctly? *Make love to others?*

"And I expect you to make love to others, too. People aren't property. How else can you strengthen your feelings for me if you don't compare me to other men?"

I could barely swallow. I finally said, "I'm going to Europe for the summer."

"Oh?" One eyebrow went up. "What an excellent idea. It will make a woman out of you."

That's not what he was supposed to say. I didn't want to go to Europe. I wanted to stay here with him. He said nothing, so I folded my arms across my chest and thought, *I'll show him.* I would become the cobra lily, prepared to strike. I'd go and he'd be sorry.

Part II

9

Deciding to Live in Paris

Armed with a guidebook and gripping my new suitcase, I stepped out of the taxi onto a cobblestone street overlooking the Seine. I had no reservation but had underlined Hotel du Pont Neuf in my *Europe on Five Dollars a Day* guidebook. It was only fifteen francs (three dollars). Fortunately, I'd been awarded a $1,500 settlement from the taxicab accident which, in 1965, was a huge amount of money. Now I could stay in cheap hotels and take trains and ferries to anywhere in Europe before returning home at the end of the summer to go to graduate school in September.

There was no hotel in sight, so I dragged the heavy suitcase to a small café where a barista was making an espresso. "Pardon," I said, *"C'est le Hotel Pont-Neuf?"* My accent was terrible even though I'd had two years of high school French. The barista looked at me blankly. I held the guidebook in her direction and pointed to the address. "Celle-ci," I said, pointing.

"*Oui oui.*" She nodded and smiled. "*Oui, ici.*"

I put down my suitcase. She said something very fast. "*Comment?*"

"What?" I said. She repeated it, even faster. I shrugged. "*Je ne comprends pas.*" I don't understand.

She came out from behind the counter, crooked her finger, indicating that I should follow, then led me through a door to the small hotel lobby, where she took my passport, wrote down my name, and put my passport in a drawer. "Hey! You can't keep my passport," I said, but she insisted it was the law, then handed me a large key with a tag that read 3. "*Ou est la salle de bains?*" I asked. Where is the bathroom?

Her eyes widened. "*Salle de bains?*"

"*Oui. Salle de bains.*" What was the big deal, anyway? Didn't the French pee?

"*Deux francs cinquante,*" she said. She wrote 2 f 50 on a small sheet of paper, handed me another key, and pointed to the staircase.

The *salle de bains* had no toilet, just a white porcelain tub and a sink. I went back downstairs and told her there was no toilet. She didn't seem to understand, so I crossed my legs and pretended to jump up and down. "*Ah, vous voulez une toilette?*" She smiled.

"*Toilette. Oui!*"

She pointed to the end of the hall.

My room was small, but two large windows opened onto a Juliette balcony overlooking the Pont Neuf, the Seine, and a small park on the tip of Isle de la Cité. Against the wall was a toilet with no seat but with a hot and cold tap. Was it a footbath? I bent closer, turned the handle, and suddenly cold water squirted up in my face. *Whoa!* A bidet! I'd read about them. French women used them for sanitary reasons, probably the same way my mother sometimes used a douche.

I flipped through the guidebook. Where first? A few weeks

ago, I'd gone to Arthur Frommer's office in New York City, and the travel agent suggested Paris, London, Rome, Florence, Athens, Nice, and back to Paris for my return flight home. I seemed to be near the Louvre, and Notre Dame was just a few blocks down the quay, the stone-faced embankment running along the Seine.

I walked in the rain to Notre Dame, which was dark and smelled like wet hair. There was no sunlight coming from the famous stained-glass windows. Disappointed and hoping at least to see the cathedral's famous gargoyles close up, I ascended a winding stairway to the balcony. Just below me, the gargoyles were vomiting rain. I looked out, hoping to see the well-known rooftops of Paris, but they were shrouded with fog. I stood there unhappily. This was Paris, the city of love, a place I didn't even want to be. And worse, I was alone.

Behind me, I heard a hissing sound and turned to face a thin, dark-haired man with Arabic features who grinned. I ignored him and went back downstairs, but he followed me, making funny smacking sounds with his lips. I pulled open the heavy door to the outside, and he was right there. I wheeled around. "Leave me alone."

"*Ecoute, mademoiselle,*" he started.

"If you don't leave me alone, I'm going to call the police." He must have understood because he didn't follow me down the street.

I went to the Louvre and walked around till I was too tired to move. Then I found a cheap restaurant not too far from the hotel. The waitress stood poised with a small pad and pencil.

"*Omelette jambon, s'il vous plait.*" The only two things I could understand on the menu were *omelette* and *biftek*, so I chose the eggs, cheaper than the beefsteak.

All the people in the restaurant were eating so strangely—fork in one hand and knife in the other. They speared their food, ate with their forks turned upside down, and never put down their knives. My omelet, which I'd expected to taste special because it was French, basically tasted the same as the ones I made back home, just less well-cooked. I scooped up the runny yolk with thick French bread. That was delicious.

I'd promised to call my mother collect to let her know I'd arrived safely, so when I got back to the hotel, I used the pay phone in the small lobby. "Oh, Margie!" She sounded relieved to hear me. I usually hated talking to her on the phone because she always sounded so needy, but this time it was different. "Are you okay, sweetie?" It was the first time she'd ever called me sweetie.

"Yes, Mom, I'm fine." Her voice sounded like a warm blanket, and I felt so alone and homesick that I began to cry. I stifled the sobs.

"I've been so worried about you. Did you find a hotel?"

"Yes, and I love it here," I lied. The tears were rolling down my cheeks.

Then she said, "I'm seeing something red, dear. Is there a red rug in your hotel room?"

I wanted to smash the receiver against the wall. "No," I yelled.

"All right, dear, you don't have to get so angry. I just saw something red and—"

"There's too much static on the line. I can't hear you," I lied, "so I'm gonna hang up."

"I love you," she said.

I took a deep breath and mumbled, "I love you, too, Mom," then hung up the phone. I think, in my entire life, this was only the second time she'd ever said I love you.

I stayed in Paris a week, visiting every attraction in the guidebook. Every few days I took the metro to American Express to check for airmail, but there was never a letter from Bob. On the morning before leaving for London, I was eating *petit dejeuner*—coffee and a baguette with butter and jam, included in my hotel price. At the table next to me was a man sipping an espresso, smoking a French cigarette, and reading a book. He looked around my age, maybe a few years older.

I stared at him and said, "Excuse me. Could you tell me how to get to the Luxembourg Gardens?" He ended up walking me there. His name was Luis, he was a Spanish painter, he spoke English, and he had come to Paris ten years ago.

"So, what do you think of Paris?" he asked, taking two cigarettes in his mouth, lighting them both, and handing one to me. It was the nicest thing anyone had done for me since I'd arrived.

"Truthfully, I'm not that crazy about Paris. That probably sounds insane, right?"

"It's not an easy city to get to know," he said. "I didn't like it when I first came, either. But it's something that grows on you, or maybe it's a matter of growing yourself. The longer you're here, you'll feel something I can't really explain."

By the time we arrived at the Luxembourg Gardens, I'd told him all about Bob and what he'd said about Europe making a woman out of me. "What do you think that means?" I asked.

Luis blew a puff of smoke into the air. "I think what he's looking for is a fine cello. And somehow, he finds you a recorder."

"A recorder?" What on earth was he talking about?

"Oh, there's nothing wrong with being a recorder," he said. "You get some very fine music, but it's not as delicate as a cello."

Luis leaned toward me, and I was going to let him kiss me, but as his lips came close, I thought I might throw up. He had foul breath, a combination of spoiled milk and cat litter. I tried to back away, but he pulled me closer with one hand, and with his other hand, tried to squeeze my breast. I swatted his hand away. He looked at me with angry, dark eyes. "You'll never be a fine cello. You're just a brass trumpet."

Back in my hotel room, I lay down on the bed and stifled my sobs into the round, hard lump they called a pillow. I opened the glass door and stood on my balcony. Here I was in the most romantic city in the world. Maybe if I could speak better French or understand what people were saying, it would be different. Well, it didn't matter because tomorrow I'd be in England, and I'd understand every word.

But as far as meeting someone was concerned, London was no

different. I visited the outside of Buckingham Palace, the Victoria and Albert Museum, and Hyde Park. I walked the streets checking out the cute guys. The English men had apple-red cheeks and excellent posture. I'd smile at the attractive guys, but no one ever smiled back.

I didn't meet anyone in London, but next was Rome, and all the great lovers came from Italy—Casanova, Romeo. I checked into my *pensione* and headed to the Borghese Gardens, which, according to my guidebook, was the most romantic place in Rome. A scooter followed me.

"*Señorita! Señorita!*"

I turned to get a look at my Italian count, a heavyset bald man, much too big for the bike. But now, because I'd turned to look, he buzzed me like a fly. I wasn't free of him until I arrived at the gardens and entered the museum.

Here I was seeing the great cities of the world, but because I'd been so hurt by Bob, all I seemed to do was concentrate on finding a guy. By the time I left Athens for Delphi and the Peloponnese, I finally began to enjoy where I was. I continued to Nice, the last stop before returning to Paris. It was late afternoon, and I was standing at the edge of the water in my yellow bikini, which I'd bought in spite of my mother's disapproval. "Margie, you can't wear that! It's indecent. It doesn't leave anything to the imagination. Return it."

"No. I'm keeping it." I'd spent days looking for a bikini. You couldn't just walk into B. Altman's and buy one. No one sold them, but I'd finally found the only store in Manhattan that had them—a dusty wholesale showroom in the garment district.

Thank God I'd refused to return it, because here, everyone wore a bikini, even middle-aged women with huge stomachs. The men wore bathing trunks as revealing as a Speedo. A very tanned guy was stacking umbrellas on the beach. He looked exactly like Bob— same-color hair, almost the same body. He saw me looking and stared back, then walked up to me and said in a thick accent, "You are American, yes?"

"How did you know?" He had Bob's eyes.

"Ah, it is obvious." He grinned, and a second later we were kissing, just like that, on the beach. After all, this was Paris, and I hadn't been kissed for three months. "You want to see where I work?" he asked. He even raised his eyebrows, just like Bob. He unlocked a door beneath the boardwalk, to which he had a key because he was the beach attendant. I followed him into a small, moldy room surrounded by piles of mattresses stacked against a wall. He slid his arms around my body, and I nuzzled his chest. He smelled like coconut suntan lotion.

"Ah cheri, cheri," he cried, moving his hand inside my bathing suit. I didn't pull away because, finally, here was a good-looking Frenchman who would take me to dinner, and he'd show me Cannes and St. Tropez and all the places I'd heard about where the rich French hung out. He threw one of the stacked mattresses to the floor, jumped on top of me, and pushed down hard on my shoulders as he tried to pry my legs apart with his hairy thighs and force himself on me.

"Hey!" I said. "Not so fast." But he paid no attention. His fist dug into my thigh as he tried to separate my legs. "You're hurting me," I yelled. I could barely breathe with his full weight on me. "Stop!" I pushed him off me and stood up.

"You American cock-tease," he spit out.

"Where's the romance?" I screamed. "I want to be made love to, not raped."

"Cock-tease."

"I am *not* a cock-tease!" I slammed the door behind me.

Bastard, I thought as I walked back to my hotel. *Forget him. Think about the good things.* After all, I'd made it through an entire summer traveling in all these foreign countries, figuring out the public transportation systems, checking into hotels where I didn't speak the language, and eating all my meals alone. I'd return to Bob sophisticated and cosmopolitan and turn him on so much that he'd beg my forgiveness and tell me how much I'd changed. He'd tell me he only wanted to be with me, exclusively.

I was on the train from Nice, returning to my little Parisian hotel.

The next day, I would fly back to New York City and begin my master's in comp lit at Columbia University. *But why?* I asked myself. I didn't want to teach and was only going for my master's because I had no life plan or man. Of course, if anyone asked, I said I intended to write a dictionary on medieval symbolism; that sounded important, and people were always impressed, but really, all I wanted to do was write.

If I returned to New York, even a tiny studio apartment would cost one hundred dollars a month, which I wouldn't be able to afford once the $1,500 ran out. Then, I'd have to live with my mother, who would nag me about when was I going to find a man and settle down, and she'd beg me to visit Kathy in the halfway house.

The entire time I'd been in Europe, I hadn't had to think about this, nor had I had the constant stomachaches as when I lived with my mother. Here, I was free of her criticisms. So why was I going home? Bob was a jerk and didn't want me, and I didn't want to go to grad school. Why not just stay? True, I didn't like Paris, but if so many people had written love stories and songs, there had to be something I was missing. Hadn't that creep at the Luxembourg Gardens told me Paris grows on you? I could stay in the cheap hotel, learn French, get a job, and find out why everyone loved Paris.

Sitting opposite me on the train was a twelve-year-old girl who lived in Manhattan and was returning to New York with her parents. I asked her, "If I give you my mother's phone number, will you call her and read a message I'm about to write?"

"Yup, I can do that," she said.

I pulled out a piece of paper and wrote, *Hi, Mom, I've decided I don't want to go to grad school. I'm going to stay in Paris, learn French, and get a job. Love, Margie.*

When I arrived back in Paris, I checked back into my little hotel, went to American Express with my plane ticket in hand, and said in as loud a voice as I dared, "Anyone want to buy a one-way plane ticket to New York for tomorrow?" Back then, you didn't need to prove you were you, you just needed a ticket to board.

"How much are you asking?" came a voice.

"One hundred dollars. That's what I paid each way. It's a charter flight."

The voice, wearing a heavy backpack, approached. "Yeah, I'll take it." He handed me five crumpled twenty-dollar bills. That would pay for over a month at my hotel, plus food and the metro without having to dip into my reserve.

The next day, my mother called person to person, figuring I'd return to the same hotel. "What do you mean, you're not coming home?" she said. "Is everything okay?"

"Yeah, Mom. Everything's fine."

"But I don't understand. I thought you wanted to get your master's?"

"Not anymore. I'm tired of school."

"Tell me the truth, dear. Are you pregnant?"

"No, Mom."

"Have you met a man?"

"I wish."

"Then why are you staying? It makes no sense."

"Because I want to see what it's like to live here."

There was a long pause. "Will you be home for Thanksgiving?"

"I doubt it."

"Will you be home for Christmas?"

"I don't know, Ma."

"Will you be home for your birthday?"

I tried not to sigh too loudly. "I have no idea."

"Well, when *will* you be home?"

"I don't know."

A long pause, then, "Do you have everything you need?"

"Yes, Mom."

"You aren't in any kind of trouble, are you?"

"Of course not."

"Does this have to do with Bob?"

"No!" I tried to keep the anger out of my voice.

"Have you told him you're staying?"

"No!"

"Do you want me to call him and tell him?"

"No!"

"Just remember that I love you and I miss you," she said softly.

"I know, Mom, I love you too." I hung up the phone, and a sob escaped. What was I doing?

10

Tiger Lily: Vincent

It was late fall. I'd now been in Paris two months, living at the Hotel du Pont Neuf for three dollars a night and taking French lessons at L'Alliance Francaise. Every day after class, I'd find a new neighborhood and meander down the cobblestone streets, listening to the laughter of children and inhaling the aroma of roasted chestnuts and jam-filled crepes. I'd look at the magnificent sand-colored buildings that hadn't changed since the sixteenth century and amble along the Seine, browsing books in the green wooden stalls that lined the banks. I'd sit at an outdoor café and drink pastis with water, eavesdropping on every conversation and trying to understand what they were saying.

I loved the Left Bank where I lived. I'd enter a small shop and say in a singsong voice the way the French did, *"Bonjour, madame."* I'd look at antique maps of Paris, hang out at the American bookstore, and go into a *patisserie* and treat myself to a sweet delight that looked like a work of art. I'd find a bench and read the *International Herald Tribune* hidden inside a copy of *Le Figaro*, because I wanted everyone to think I was French.

Now, I could finally order more than an *omelette* or *bifteck*. It might be *gratinée de coquille St. Jacques*, a shrimp and scallop dish, or *emincé de volaille sauce Roquefort avec pommes de terre sautées*, thin slices of fillet of chicken with Roquefort sauce and sautéed potatoes. All the things that had seemed so strange, like co-ed bathrooms, were now part of my life. If a man was in the *toilette* washing his hands, I'd smile, go into a stall, and flush the toilet so he couldn't hear anything.

I'd also learned how to eat without having to put down my knife each time I cut meat. If I saw Americans switching their silverware from hand to hand, I'd think, *Moi, la petite français*—me, the little French girl. On Saturdays, I'd take the bottle of chilled wine from my bidet, slip it into a string shopping bag, and go to the boulangerie with its heady smell of fresh-baked bread. *"Merci, madame,"* I'd say as the owner handed me a warm baguette. I might add, *"Le temps fait beau,"* the weather is beautiful, or *"Quel dommage qu'il pluvait hier,"* what a pity it rained yesterday. I'd slip the baguette in my bag and pronounce in my singsong voice just like the French, *"Au revoir, madame."*

At the *epicerie*, I'd say, *"S'il vous plait, choissez une brie bon courrant pour moi,"* choose me a good runny brie. I was so proud that I knew runny meant ripe. After, I'd go to the little park under the Pont Neuf and eat lunch while listening to the Seine lap against the bank. Sometimes, a *bateau mouche* boat would arrive, and as the tourists disembarked, I'd look at them smugly because I lived here. I belonged, and they were just tourists. And then I'd light up a *gitane sans filtre* trying not to gag on the black tobacco I could barely stomach but knew made me look more French.

The French women had a reputation as the most beautiful women in the world, but they were actually quite plain. They carried themselves elegantly and dressed chicly with perfect hair and makeup.

What made them beautiful was they always had the right dress, the right shoes and purse, and even the right makeup to cover any flaws. Unlike American women, they didn't try to show everything off; they only emphasized their best feature. For instance, if a woman had a gorgeous neck, she'd wear something low-cut to draw attention to it.

None of the French had long, straight hair halfway down their back. My hair had always been short and curly, but it had grown so long it was now straight and I didn't want to cut it. Often, I wore it in a ponytail, thinking that made me look more French. I practiced walking, because French women walked differently; they swung their hips more. I'd follow a woman in the Tuileries Gardens and imitate her movements. Still, the women looked different—it was the way they dressed, not like my practical, drip-dry travel clothes.

One day, my mother sent me an unexpected check: "Feel free to use this for an airplane ticket," her letter said. Instead, I went into a boutique on the Left Bank, where the saleswoman sold me a white wool turtleneck and a gray flannel Courrèges skirt with white piping. To match the outfit, I bought white go-go boots. The clothes cost as much as a transatlantic plane ticket.

"How do the French afford these expensive clothes?" I asked the saleswoman.

"American women have to have different clothes for every day of the week," she said, "but French women buy only one or two new outfits and wear them the entire season." I would wear my new outfit till it fell apart, just like the French.

And then, miracle of all miracles—through the expat community, I managed to get a good-paying job with a company that dubbed foreign films into English. My job was to set up the schedules and cast the actors who dubbed the voices into English. I was good at my job because of my summer experience stage managing. Happily, my boss thought so, too, because he got me a green card. Now I *really* belonged. Every morning, I'd board the metro and get off at my stop on the Champs Elysée, walk around the Rond-Point and swing my hips just like the French women.

One day, I met an Englishman having breakfast in my hotel's

café. He was just visiting from London, but his good friend was an American expat who lived here. Did I want him to set me up on a blind date? The blind date's name was Vincent, and he'd worked for Bernie Cornfeld at IOS, a Switzerland-based mutual fund company. Along with a few of his coworkers, Vincent had retired at forty years old, a millionaire, and now lived in Paris. Forty was much too old for me, but maybe he'd know a French guy my age. I was to meet him at his Montparnasse apartment for a drink, and then we'd go to La Coupole for dinner.

Vincent had a bushy red beard, mustache, and bright-red hair. He reminded me of a tiger lily, a plant whose orange flower petals are curved and speckled with dark spots, a plant that represents wealth. His teeth were pointy, and he had small slits for eyes. His hawkish nose made him look angry, definitely not my type. But Vincent had a gentle, unassuming manner and didn't seem the least bit conceited, the way I expected a rich guy to be. His apartment was spacious with a wrap-around terrace overlooking the iconic Paris rooftops and with the Eiffel Tower in the distance. I sank into a plushy brown leather Eames chair, and he handed me a glass of twelve-year-old Ambassador Scotch. He clinked my glass against his and said, "If you're going to drink Scotch, it should be the best." The liquid slid down my throat but didn't burn the way Scotch usually did.

At La Coupole, the maître d' directed us to the right side, the fancy side with tablecloths.

"*Non, non, monsieur,*" Vincent said firmly. "*Ici.*" He pointed to the left side with paper tablecloths, then whispered to me, "Only the tourists dine on the right."

A waiter's tray crashed to the ground, and the entire restaurant burst into applause. What fun! Vincent told me this was a favorite place of Hemingway and Jean Cocteau and F. Scott Fitzgerald. I wondered if one of them had sat at our very table. A woman selling red roses stood over us.

"*Trois francs,*" she said.

Vincent reached into his pocket, handed her a five-franc note, and told her to keep the change. He handed me the rose, and said, "To a beautiful woman." Neither Gordy nor Bob had ever bought me flowers or said I was beautiful.

Vincent seemed to know everyone. People came over to pay him homage, and he introduced me as "my new friend, a recent expat." And then he looked at me as though he'd discovered something precious. His friends picked up on this and nodded their approval to Vincent. He introduced me to a famous French artist and a French producer in whose play Vincent had invested. A gallery owner invited Vincent to a *vernissage*, a gallery opening, and a famous designer, Bob Gill, showed Vincent a sample of stationery he was creating with Vincent's name and street address embossed on a design of a bright-blue Paris street sign.

"Do you like oysters?" Vincent asked.

"I love oysters!" I lied. I'd never had them in my life but knew they were expensive and had heard they were an aphrodisiac, if there really was such a thing. The waiter placed an enormous metal tray full of oysters on the table and then returned with a small bowl of something that looked like salad dressing. I said to Vincent, "Can you ask the waiter to bring us some cocktail sauce?"

Vincent whispered, "The French never put cocktail sauce on oysters. Just squeeze some lemon and dunk them into this red vinaigrette sauce."

I watched Vincent squeeze the lemon, then stab an oyster with a tiny fork, dip it into the vinaigrette sauce, and pop it into his mouth. I did the same, but paused before swallowing because it looked slimy. The oyster slithered down my throat—sweet and much tastier than clams. Then the *steak au poivre* arrived, a chunk of beef thicker than my fist. I'd asked for medium, but Vincent suggested I order it *saignant*, even though I never ate rare steak. "You can savor the flavors better when it's not so well done," he said.

I was beginning to feel like Eliza Doolittle. And he was right—the steak was excellent. Was it because it was so rare, or was it the pepper sauce? Victor told me he was from Chicago but planned to stay in Paris for the rest of his life because he loved skiing in Europe. It was such an easy flight to get to the Alps, he said. He'd rented a ski chalet for the season in Zermatt, Switzerland, and would go there as soon as the slopes opened. Vincent ordered Calvados, a French apple brandy as popular to the French as beer is to Americans. He clinked his glass against mine and said, "To many more delightful evenings together."

He was charming, worldly, and considerate. I'd had a lot to drink, so I was feeling warm and cuddly. His hand rested on the table, and I slid mine toward his and touched his pinkie. I didn't feel any chemistry. Nothing. Actually, his little finger almost felt clammy. I could hear my mother's voice, "Better to marry a prince than a pauper," and my grandmother, who'd always say, "Do you want to be poor all your life?"

Look where attraction had gotten me—Gordy the bastard and Bob the cheat. Maybe attraction wasn't the answer, maybe caring was. Who cared if there was no chemistry? Perhaps it would come in time. This was the first man I'd met who not only took a real interest in me but also came with an entire cadre of friends. It had been a long time since I'd felt part of a group.

A few days later, Vincent took me to dinner at a fancy restaurant in the Bois du Boulogne in his Rover—not a Land Rover, but a shiny gray sedan that looked like a cross between a Jaguar and a Rolls-Royce I sat on the buttery leather seat, which tilted back with the touch of a finger. It was like sitting on a moveable throne. The interior smelled like new leather. I'd never been in a new car before. My father had always bought Ford sedans secondhand, at least five years old.

We were stopped at a red light in front of the Pont Alexandre III, an ornate golden bridge that looked like a lit-up castle. Vincent took his hand off the steering wheel and put it on my knee. I'm ticklish there, so I jumped. My father used to squeeze my knee, teasing me, and the more I screamed for him to stop, the more he would squeeze. It drove me crazy.

Vincent asked, "How would you like to go away with me next weekend? I know a beautiful little hotel with a three-Michelin-starred restaurant just a few hours from Paris. I've wanted to go there for a while."

I'd never stayed in a fancy hotel or eaten in a three-star restaurant, but would that mean I'd be obligated to sleep with him? Obviously, he wasn't talking about separate rooms. I couldn't imagine making love with him, but no one had ever treated me so well. And maybe he was a fabulous lover!

Our suite at the elegant inn, sumptuous enough to be Marie Antoinette's bedroom, had a four-poster canopy bed and exquisite antique furniture. We strolled around the gardens and had a glass of champagne at the wood-paneled bar before walking arm in arm into the candlelit dining room. I'd never before been to a restaurant with such fine linen tablecloths.

"Look," Vincent whispered. "You're turning every head in the room."

The waiter handed us two oversized menus. The first item under appetizers was *foie gras with truffles*, which I'd never had before and knew had to cost a bundle, but my menu had no prices.

"So, what will you have?" I couldn't see Vincent because of the vase of pink and white roses, which he moved to the side. I wanted to try the foie gras, but not unless I knew the price. I didn't need to know because Vincent ordered for us both. The waiter set down two Limoges plates, each holding a thick slice of foie gras with black truffles. I watched Vincent spread some on a toast point and followed his lead. How could anything be this delicious?

"Boy," he grinned, "they really must have had to hold back those pigs."

"What pigs?"

"For the truffles. They take pigs into the forest to sniff, and they dig them out."

"You're joking, right?"

"No! The pigs find the truffles, and they try to eat them, so the farmers have to hold them back with a staff."

The waiter reappeared with two enormous steaming bowls of *bouillabaisse* in which floated chunks of lobster, shellfish, fish, and vegetables. For dessert, we each had a *soufflé* with bubbling-hot chocolate Grand Marnier sauce.

By the time we walked up the flight of stairs to our suite, I was giddy from the rich food and wine. The room smelled like rose petals. The maid had folded up the bedspread onto an upholstered stool, and resting on each bed pillow was a chocolate. Vincent went into the bathroom and brushed his teeth. He'd just spent a fortune on the meal, not to mention what the room must have cost. I knew what was expected of me.

I thought about my time at Columbia, when an assistant professor I was briefly dating had cooked dinner, starting by soaking fresh beans for four hours. Then he'd made hummus and two other delicious dishes, after which he took me into the bedroom and we took off our clothes. But there was no chemistry. I apologized that I had a horrible stomachache, threw my clothes back on, and took the subway home. When I told my mother, she said, "Awww, he cooked for you all day long. The least you could have done was sleep with him."

Now, dreading what was about to happen, I took off my clothes. Should I lie naked on the bed? Under the covers? Should I sit on the armchair and cover myself provocatively with pillows? I tried posing on the bed. I'd never lain on sheets this silky. Vincent was taking a long time. Was he looking for condoms? Should I tell him I had an IUD? The door finally opened. He stood there in a fluffy terrycloth hotel robe. "God, you're beautiful," he said.

He slipped off his robe as he approached the bed. His skin was very pale. He was wearing white droopy underwear and hadn't taken off his black socks. He lay down on the bed and said nothing but looked me up and down, though he made no attempt to touch me. Maybe he was just shy? Should I make the first move? I kissed him, but his beard was bristly and hurt my skin. I moved my head to his belly, which smelled of expensive soap. He didn't seem interested. I tried everything, but no response.

Finally, I said, "Is it me?" I knew full well it wasn't.

"No, I have a headache," he said. "Maybe we should just go to sleep."

He gave me a peck on the cheek and rolled over to his side. I could hear the nightstand clock: *tick, tick, tick*. I wanted to get up and take a steaming bubble bath. Darn. If only he'd swept me off my feet. Maybe he didn't like sex, but I wanted a lover, not a brother. I would stop seeing him when we returned to Paris.

Driving back home, Vincent explained there was a five-day French holiday coming up. Did I want to go skiing with him in Zermatt? I thought about Gordy standing me up that time in college.

"I've never skied before, and I don't have ski clothes." My ski pants and parka, never worn, were back in my mother's apartment in New York City.

"Don't worry. I'll buy you an outfit and rent your equipment."

"But I'd hold you up. I'd be slow."

"Oh no," he laughed. "I won't ski with you! I'll ski with my friends and put you in ski school. We'll meet for lunch and dinner." How could I say no? I'd go, just this one time. And after that, I'd tell him we weren't right for each other.

Maybe we weren't right for each other, but Zermatt was right for me. I loved being outside looking at snow-covered mountains higher than I'd ever seen, surrounded by tall pine trees blanketed in white. I loved smelling the crispness of the air and feeling wet, cold snowflakes hit my cheeks or the sun warming my face. After the first day in ski school, there wasn't an inch on my body that wasn't black and blue from falling, but I didn't care. A day later, I made my first snowplow turn. My class advanced to a hill a touch higher than the bunny slope.

"Let's go!" the instructor called out as we followed him down the hill. "Bend zee knees."

We went back up the chair lift and all was silent except the *clink*

clink of the lift as it passed the steel poles, then silence again, then *whoosh* as a skier flew down the hill beneath us. It was magical.

For lunch, I'd unlace my rigid leather ski boots (back then you laced them up) and *clomp clomp* into the dining room to join Vincent and his friends. After lunch, I'd return to ski school. At night, we ate out, often fondue into which we dipped pieces of bread or steak. Then, we'd return to the chalet and crawl into the same bed, but it wasn't often that he wanted to make love. If he wasn't claiming a headache, it was a stomach virus or asthma.
I knew he wasn't gay. Occasionally, he'd touch me, and every now and then make love to me, but he never said anything or made a sound. I imagined myself with a handsome Frenchman my age having awesome sex. Vincent could never be that man. Worse, every time he pulled out his wallet and paid for another expensive meal, I felt guilty. Wherever we went, he'd slip his arm through mine with that proud look, and I knew he was my sugar daddy. I was his arm candy.

When we returned to Paris, I learned that my fabulous cheap hotel was going to be turned into apartments, and we had three weeks to vacate. I looked for a new place, but everything was either too expensive or an eighth-floor walkup. Plus, it was impossible to get an apartment with a telephone unless you were willing to pay five hundred dollars key money.

Vincent and I sat at the Café de Flores. "I don't know what to do," I said. "I've looked everywhere."

"So why don't you move in with me?" he said.

I knew it wasn't the right thing to do, but what if I moved in for just a few months? I moved in, and soon after he surprised me with my own stationery, just like his, with my name and *55 Avenue du Maine* in royal blue letters. He was spoiling me. He didn't expect me to cook, either. He'd invite six friends to lunch, slap a huge stack of French francs in my hand, and send me out to the most expensive *épicerie* to buy patés and cheeses and leeks. I'd make a salad with garlic dressing, and Vincent's friends would tell me how delicious everything was, as if I'd been slaving in the kitchen all morning.

We returned to Zermatt for Christmas, and Vincent bought me brand-new Head skis, poles, ski boots with buckles instead of laces, and a week's worth of ski school lessons. This time, I learned how to make parallel turns and graduated to the advanced beginner class, then the intermediate class. I loved skiing as much as I loved tennis. All I had to do was keep Vincent company, and he was happy. I was disappointed he didn't want a physical relationship, but how could I not want to be with a guy who was so generous and always complimented me, something no one had ever done before.

It was our last night in Zermatt. We were in a restaurant and Vincent toasted with *Chateauneuf du Pape*. "Here's to you." He smiled. "You've really taken so well to skiing, and you're advancing so quickly. I can barely believe you just started. Why don't you quit your job and stay here for the rest of the season? I'll buy you a season pass, and all you have to do is babysit the chalet."

I gasped. "You mean, stay here and ski? Alone?"

"Oh no," he chuckled. "You're not ready to ski alone. I'll buy you ski school for the rest of the season."

"Why won't you be here?"

"I have too much going on, but I'll fly in weekends."

Stay here with free room and board and ski lessons? I thought about my job in Paris where, basically, I was just an assistant to bad actors who thought they were movie stars. I called my boss, quit my job, and stayed in Zermatt through spring, skiing the glaciers and black diamonds in the most advanced class. I didn't feel lonely. I was at peace with the majesty and silence of the mountains. When the season ended, I returned to Vincent's apartment. He told me he'd found a huge atelier (artist's studio) on the Rue du Val du Grace, and I was welcome to come with him.

The atelier was spectacular, a spacious loft with an open kitchen, enormous living and dining areas, three bedrooms upstairs around a balcony, and a third-floor attic with a sunbathing roof. Vincent was rarely around, so I had the place to myself; but I was tired of being kept by a sugar daddy and didn't want to go through all my accident settlement money, so I networked the expats until I finally found a new freelance job.

Agnes was French, bilingual, and needed someone who could write English words on a transparent piece of film, which the actors would later dub in a studio. This included little screams, which I wrote as "Ahhhh," or big ones, which I wrote as "AHHHHHHHHHHHH." It was a temporary job, but I loved it and worked from home at the dining room table. One day, Vincent called from Geneva. Francoise Truffaut, the famous director of *The 400 Blows* and *Jules et Jim* was looking for an atelier to shoot his next film and would be coming by that afternoon.

A few hours later, Francois Truffaut showed up with his production designer. He was shooting a new film with Jeanne Moreau called *La Mariée était en Noir* (The Bride Wore Black) and wanted to shoot in the atelier for four days.

"*Bien sur,*" I said. He noticed the piece of film on which I'd been writing and asked what it was. Did he really not know? I explained it was for dubbing, that it was the *band mere*, the film strip that ran along the bottom of the screen so an actor could sync up the words with the picture. Truffaut seemed fascinated.

A month later, Truffaut returned with an entire crew and lights and cables and camera, and cast, including Jeanne Moreau. I tried not to stare. She looked exactly as she did in her movies. I watched the filming from the living room couch. Jeanne Moreau was dressed in a short white hunting dress and held a bow and arrow, which she'd later use to kill the artist. I'd watch till I was bored, then I'd go up to the attic and bang away on my portable Brother typewriter, working on my novel.

The day Vincent returned, Truffaut had hired a dozen or so *figurants* (extras) for a party scene in the atelier. He asked if Vincent and I wanted to be in the film. (If you stream the film on Amazon Prime, you'll see me in a tight orange sweater, long straight hair to my butt, and bell-bottom wool pants.) In the scene, we were to mingle, but the second I saw where the camera was placed, I walked right up to the actor, Jean-Claude Brialy. A second later, I was blocked by another actor.

"Coupee!" Truffaut called. "Margie," he said in French. "That was brilliant! Can you do it again?" I had no idea what I'd done, but again, I approached Brialy. It wasn't the same as before. After the third take, Truffaut gave up.

Every Friday, Truffaut hosted a "wrap party" at a nearby French café, to which Vincent and I were invited. It was June 1967, the first day of the Israeli war against Egypt, Syria, and Jordan. Jean-Claude told me if the war continued, he would quit the film and go fight for Israel. Fortunately, he didn't have to, because the war lasted only six days.

Truffaut invited Vincent and me to be extras at a cemetery funeral scene. All the women wore appropriate black dresses, but I had no black dress, so I wore my royal-blue dress with a thick black belt. I tried not to walk with Vincent because I didn't want to be caught forever with him on film. As we did take after take walking to the burial plot, all I could think of was that I wanted to find a permanent new job and get my own apartment. This arrangement wasn't working.

A few weeks later, my freelance assignment was over, and I told a fellow expat I was looking for a job. "I know the perfect person," he said. "Call John Berry. He's a film director making a new movie and needs an assistant." It would be the beginning of a completely different life in Paris—creative and thrilling.

11

Chameleon: John

I sat on a Queen Anne armchair in the lobby bar of the Prince de Galles Hotel on the Avenue George V, waiting for American expat director John Berry, who had started his career working for Orson Welles. Berry had been blacklisted and escaped to Paris to avoid testifying before the House Un-American Activities Committee. A fiftyish man looking like a curly dark-haired version of Chico Marx came toward me. Wearing a brown suede jacket pulled up at the collar, he swaggered like a boxer and extended his hand. "Hi, I'm John Berry." There was something reassuring about his voice.

He didn't just look like Chico Marx. He looked like my father, except his eyes weren't sad or angry. John's eyes sparkled. If he were a plant, he'd be a chameleon, a bright and flashy groundcover that grows in poor or wet soil and has to be kept under control, as it gets out of hand quickly.

John told me he was writing a screenplay called *Á Tout Casser*, Break Everything Up, which he hoped to finish in two months and then shoot in Paris. He was looking for an assistant who spoke French to whom he could dictate the script, and he wanted to start right away. His voice was deep, and he had a thick New York accent, the kind that normally bothered me (but not his).

"Can you type?" he asked.

"Yes, with two fingers, but I'm really fast. I can type one hundred words a minute." I had no idea how many words I could actually type, but I wanted this job.

"Good," he said. "And you're free to start right away?"

"I can start right now if you want." *Did he just hire me?*

"I originally turned this screenplay down." He spoke with his hands, the way my father used to do. "The producer wanted it to be a second-rate *policier* movie, know what I mean?" I nodded. "I don't do B movies. I didn't get blacklisted just to do those," he said. "I'll only do something that has meaning." He didn't speak, he orated. His lips were large and sensual. "But when the producer said Johnny Hallyday was the star, that changed everything."

Johnny Hallyday? My mouth hung open. Hallyday was the Elvis Presley of Paris, with more than a dozen platinum albums.

"Will Sylvie Vartan be in it too?" I asked. Vartan, also a famous singer, was married to Hallyday. I wanted John to know I was not just some dumb, starstruck American girl, but a sophisticated expat who knew things. Like how I knew Chez Regine was the hottest club on the Left Bank, though there was no way to work that into the conversation.

"When I knew they had Hallyday, I told the producer I'd do it if he'd let me rewrite the script," said John. "I want to turn it into a modern French western with cowboys on motorcycles chased by a vegetarian Mafioso chief." He sat up in his chair and said in a funny accent, "So vat is so meaningful about dat? Meaning, schmeaning, you schmuck. Johnny Hallyday. *That's* your meaning."

John was funny. I'd never met anyone like him. He returned to his normal voice. "You free to start on Monday?"

"Absolutely!" This was my ticket to freedom from Vincent.

"Do you have a place we could work?" he asked. "We could work at my house, but it's in Sèvres, a half-hour train ride away, so it would be easier to work here in Paris."

Perfect timing. Vincent had just left to visit his mother in Chicago and would be gone for at least three weeks. I'd worry later about what to do when he returned. "We can work at my place," I said.

"Okay, then we're all set." His eyes smiled. He just seemed so joyous. He reached out to shake my hand. Neither of us stood up, nor did he release my hand. Finally, he said, "Maybe you'd like to have dinner tonight so we can discuss this further?"

"I'd love to," I said. We exchanged phone numbers. I was walking on air.

I lingered in the tub, soaking in the expensive French bubble bath I allowed myself on special occasions. I brushed on three layers of mascara so I'd look like Brigitte Bardot. I put on a ton of blush, just like Twiggy in a Mary Quant ad. I slipped on the cute Courrèges outfit and pulled on my white leather boots. Maybe he wasn't French, and obviously he was much older than me, but that didn't matter because this was Paris, where no one cared. He was funny, charming, and smart. Not only was I going to have this fabulous job, but I had a feeling there was something else going on between us.

It was early, so I went up to the attic and looked out at Paris's rooftops. Sometimes they looked gray and gloomy, but tonight they were silhouetted against a sky painted in bold strokes of orange and red. In the distance, the Eiffel Tower twinkled as if studded with diamonds. Now I'd finally have someone to share all of this with. Okay, he was American, but he'd lived here long enough to qualify as French. And besides, he spoke much better French than me. He'd ask me to move in with him, and we'd do everything together. No more having to go to the American movies all alone.

At 6 p.m. he hadn't called. He had specifically said dinner tonight. *Should I get dressed and wait for him downstairs? He doesn't have my address!* I felt hot. If I weren't careful, I'd sweat off all my makeup. I thumbed through old issues of *Paris Match* but couldn't concentrate. I could barely read the photo captions. Twenty minutes passed. Seven p.m. came and went. Maybe he'd lost my phone number? I pulled the slip of paper from my purse and picked up the receiver. There was no dial tone. The phone was dead.

I raced down the street to the Tabac to the pay phone, anxiously inserted the *jeton* coin, and dialed. *Beep beep beep beep* — the familiar sound meant the phone would now ring. I pushed the button and listened as the *jeton* clinked inside the phone box. It rang once. Twice. Three times. A female voice picked up. "Hello?" She sounded American. *He's married?* I slammed down the phone. Had I completely misjudged this? I walked home, put on my nightgown, and crawled into bed.

The next morning, the persistent ring of the phone woke me. "Hey!" John said. "You stood me up last night! I kept calling you and never got an answer."

"I'm so sorry, the phone was broken. I kept waiting for you to call. I thought you stood *me* up!"

"How about a rain check tonight?"

I couldn't say yes fast enough.

We sat at a small café sipping Beaujolais. I wasn't sure if it was the wine or the warm glow from the lights or our knees almost touching under the table. Maybe it was the way he'd taken the corner of his napkin and dabbed a little smudge of butter from my lip after I'd eaten an escargot. He made me feel special, not like some ornament, the way I felt with Vincent.

Maybe we could never be together on a permanent basis since he was married, but maybe we could have an affair. After all, this was Paris, and he was suave, worldly, and sophisticated. After a while, I finally had the courage to say, "So, when I didn't hear from you last night, I called your house. Your wife answered. I didn't know what to say, so I hung up." I looked at him. Would he try to deny it? Hadn't Bob denied there was anything going on with that slut who wrote him a love letter?

He laughed easily. "Oh! That was Gladys! Why didn't you just ask for me?"

So, he *was* married. "I was too embarrassed. I mean, I don't just call up a man's house and ask his wife to speak to her husband."

He laughed again. "Gladys and I have been divorced for ten years."

"How can you be divorced if you *live* with each other?" I asked.

"I don't live with Gladys. I live in a tiny cottage behind the big house. Before, we all lived in the big house and rented out the cottage, but when we divorced, I moved into the cottage and Gladys stayed in the big house with the children—well, neither one's so much a child right now. Jan's twenty-seven. I think she'll be a professional student for the rest of her life." I realized Jan was two years older than me. "And Denny is twenty-five. He's a filmmaker, *really* talented."

My age, I thought. John was twenty-seven years older than me.

He said, "You know how impossible it is to find an apartment in Paris? That's why I still live there. I have to pay her alimony, unfortunately, for the rest of her life, and the cottage is much cheaper than an apartment in Paris." He looked at me and smiled. "You didn't have to hang up on Gladys. She understands everything."

I wanted to believe him, but it sounded fishy. "Uh, if you have your own place, how come you share the phone?"

"Because it's impossible to get a phone line in Paris, and it's even worse in the suburbs. You can wait five years to buy a line. When the call is for me, Gladys calls out from the back door, and I go across the lawn to answer it."

It was true about trying to get a phone. He said he and Gladys had fallen in love when he was just twenty-one, apprenticing for Orson Welles at the Mercury Theatre. He puffed out his chest and said dramatically, "I was a very important actor. I was a spear carrier in *Julius Caesar*, a crucial role. I even had a line, 'What ho, my Lord!'" He waited for me to stop laughing. "Of course, I wanted to play Marc Antony, but I auditioned for John Houseman and he said, 'You're a splendid fellow, but your New York accent is dreadful. I suggest elocution lessons.'"

In 1942, when he was twenty-five years old, he played a defense lawyer in Orson's production of Richard Wright's *Native Son*. "My father gave me two choices," he said. "'You can be a boxer or an actor.' I chose actor." His voice changed and he went into a new routine. "The big famous actor, John Berry—which, by the way, wasn't my name then. It was Jack Sold, but I changed it to John Berry because I'd heard of the Duc du Berry, and Jack Sold don't sound like a matinee idol, right? Vat? Starring Jackie Szold?"

I'd never known a man who could make me laugh so much except my father when he wasn't in a rage. John had all the good parts of my father—the funny, charming part—but he didn't seem like someone who lost his temper the way my father did. John was strong, kind of like Paul Bunyan with brains. And his life was fascinating.

"Tell me about Orson," I said.

"Oh, Orson." He sat back and knitted his hands on the back of his head. "Orson was a genius. A brilliant, brilliant director. Working with him was like living in the center of a volcano. Exciting and glamorous and full of the kind of theatricality that lasts forever. And. He. Spoke. Like. This. Before I was Orson's assistant, I wanted to act, but after, I wanted to direct, so I left for Hollywood in 1944."

The same year I was born, I thought.

"Houseman really believed in me, so he helped me get my first film. I was twenty-three years old. It was called *Miss Susie Slagle's*, and it starred Lillian Gish, Veronica Lake, Joan Caulfield, and Sonny Tufts. After that, I directed John Garfield and Shelley Winters in *He Ran All the Way*, and then the House Un-American Activities Committee, doing a witch hunt on Hollywood's entertainment industry, came looking for me." I knew about HUAC from American History.

"Do you know about the Hollywood Ten?" he asked. I knew there were ten Hollywood screenwriters and film directors accused of being Communists and who were supposed to testify before HUAC. "With HUAC," John said, "you had three choices." He lit a cigarette, handed it to me, and lit another one for himself. I loved that. "Once someone snitched on you," he said, "you could testify and name names, like Gadge Kazan did, the fink."

I looked at him funny and he said, "Elia Kazan, the director of *On the Waterfront*. He named names, the bastard. Or you could flee, like Dalton Trumbo, who went to Mexico. You could also plead the fifth and choose jail. I was making a film about the Hollywood Ten, and that didn't sit well with HUAC. And then someone testified that I'd held a cell meeting at my house." He paused.

"So, what happened?" I was on the edge of my chair.

"Well, I'd trained Gladys never to answer the door without looking through the peephole first. When the FBI came knocking, she stalled them long enough for me to grab my passport and the suitcase I always had ready. I jumped out the ground-floor window in the back of the house and ran till I found a taxi to the airport. That's how I got to Paris. Later, she came with the kids. And then, as I told you, I got divorced. I've now been here eighteen years."

He was an encyclopedia of experiences. "So why did you get divorced?" I asked.

"I guess I just fell out of love," he said. "I don't know—maybe it was the whole HUAC thing. I still think of Gladys fondly, after all, I was married to her a long time. But I don't have the same feelings I once had. You'll meet her. You'll like her." He looked into my eyes. "How about you? Are you with someone?"

"Well." I let out a small sigh. Was he seeing a future for us the way I was? "I live with this guy, Vincent. We have a kind of strange relationship. I mean, it's like living with your brother." He gave me a funny look, not the flirty kind he'd been giving me all night, so I said, "I'm ready to end it with Vincent. He's in Chicago right now. He'll be gone for three weeks."

We got into a taxi, and I gave the driver my address. Had I made the bed? We drove along the Seine. It was dark, but the water had an iridescent sheen. The bridges sparkled like constellations of stars. *This* was the Paris of love I'd never seen before. He reached over and kissed me. I inhaled the faint aroma of his French aftershave.

He undressed me slowly on Vincent's bed, touching me in a way I'd never experienced before. After, I lay cradled in his arms, my head against his damp chest hairs. Tears ran down my face.

He sat up. "What's the matter?"

"I don't know. I just feel so . . . happy!"

"Oh, thank God," he said, kissing me again. "I thought maybe you were regretting being with me in Vincent's bed."

I burst out laughing. "Are you serious? What we did is exactly what this bed needed."

John shook his head. "There has to be something wrong with Vincent. No one in his right mind wouldn't want to touch you." He stroked the inside of my arm. How would I ever again sleep in this bed with Vincent?

12

Life with John

John and I worked on his script at Vincent's atelier. John didn't just dictate. I'd fling out ideas, and if I suggested something particularly funny, he'd throw his arms around me and say, "Oh, that's perfect! You're such a good writer." No one except my fourth-grade teacher had ever praised my writing, not even my parents. "Writing is not a career," my father said. "How will you support yourself?" My father hated his own writing, but John loved his and mine. When we finished our first scene, John said, "Oh, that is so good. Let's celebrate." He took a small, balled-up piece of tin foil from his pocket and unrolled a brown square about the size of a bouillon cube.

"What's that?" I asked.

"Hashish. I mix it with weed. A wonderful high."

I'd tried marijuana in college, but never hashish. All marijuana made me do was eat endless peanut-butter-and-jam sandwiches on Wonder Bread.

"Is this safe?" It felt like something my mother would ask, but I would never be like my mother. I wouldn't marry a man who couldn't support his family. I would write screenplays with John and they'd be huge box office hits.

"Of course it's safe!" John stuck a pin in the cube and held a match to it. "You're gonna love it," he said as he crumpled the softened hashish in his fingers, sprinkled it into a joint with weed, lit it, took a deep drag, and handed it to me. I tried not to cough. "Have another toke," he said. Everything began to feel silky and warm. John looked at me and grinned. "Come on, let's go for a walk."

We sat on green folding chairs at the Jardin du Luxembourg next to the pond, where children prodded toy sailboats with sticks. I'd never sat quietly like this with anyone before. This had to be what love was—having someone with whom you didn't even have to talk.

Three weeks flew by. When we worked on the script, often he'd massage my shoulders or kiss the back of my neck and my spine would tingle. I'd never been so happy. And then, a postcard came from Vincent: *"I'll be home Wednesday, Air France, 6:00 a.m. Can't wait to see you."*

What would we do now? John gathered up his things into a leather duffel bag. He'd been quiet all morning. Finally, he lit a joint, took a drag, and handed it to me. "Why don't we just get an apartment together?" He said, "It's ridiculous not to rent out the little house when I'm never there, and you said you're ready to move from here. What do you think?" I flung my arms around him.

The next day, we had lunch with a famous French actor friend of John's, Claude Dauphin. Dauphin knew of a three-month sublet with a telephone on the Rue Jean Goujon directly opposite the St.

Regis Hotel. The apartment on a beautiful tree-lined street looked like the vine-covered home that Madeline lived in with the other eleven orphans in Ludwig Bemelmans's book. Shafts of sunlight fell across the wide-planked wooden floors. The kitchen was stocked with every possible pot, pan, and utensil. Maybe I could learn to cook like Julia Child. We left, thrilled, but suddenly I felt this horrible pit in my stomach. How would I tell Vincent?

My mother's mantra was always, "Never hurt anyone's feelings." Vincent had done nothing to hurt me, and I had no idea what to say. That night, I went to sleep and woke up at 5 a.m. I sat drinking coffee until a key turned in the lock and Vincent entered. He put down his suitcase.

"Oh," he said. "I thought you'd be sound asleep."

I made myself smile. "Welcome home!" I said. I hugged him and he gave me a little peck on the lips. His mustache was scratchy as usual. He threw his trench coat on the couch. "How was the trip?" I asked.

"Good. Mom's fine. My sister's fine. Everyone's well." He kept looking at me and then said, "You look . . . absolutely radiant. What have you been up to? I've never seen you look this beautiful."

There was no *way* he could know. "Well, um . . . I found a job," I said.

"Good for you!" He looked proud. "What kind of job?"

"Working as the creative assistant for John Berry."

"Oh, the director?" He pulled on his beard.

"Yes," I said.

"That's nice." He took a bottle of twelve-year-old Ambassador Scotch from a duty-free bag and smiled. "I'm replacing the stock. We were just about out."

I went on. "And uh . . . I uh . . . I've found an apartment."

"Oh?" He squinted at me. "I didn't know you were looking."

"Well, I wasn't looking . . . I mean . . . I wasn't looking *before* I found the job. I mean . . . uh." I swallowed and said, "I've fallen in love with John Berry, and we're taking an apartment together."

He looked surprised. "That was sudden, wasn't it?"

"It just kind of happened."

"Oh." He ran his hand through his hair. "I see." He wouldn't look me in the eye.

Maybe I'd been wrong about him. Maybe I meant more to him than arm candy and he was just a guy who couldn't express his feelings. He put the Scotch inside the liquor cabinet. "Well, I wish you luck."

"Do you want me to leave right now?" I asked.

He made a strange sound, almost a sob. "No, you can stay as long as you want."

I felt so guilty. Here I'd been living in his apartment, skiing all winter at his condo in Zermatt, and eating expensive meals on his dime. That night, after we'd shared almost half a bottle of Ambassador Scotch, I slept with Vincent in his bed for the last unhappy time.

Two months later, John and I sat in bumper-to-bumper traffic on the Ring Road surrounding Paris. He'd now been shooting the film for almost five weeks, and we were on our way to the location for a chase scene between Johnny Hallyday on motorcycle and the gangsters in pickup trucks.

John slapped his knee. "*Merde!* We're gonna be so late, I *hate* being late."

I patted his knee. "It's okay, sweetie, they can't start without you." I loved being stuck in traffic because it was one of the few times I had him to myself. The moment we arrived, everyone on the set needed him: the cameraman, the lighting designer, the prop man, the makeup artist, but especially Johnny Hallyday, who demanded constant handholding. The co-star, Eddie Constantine, an American expat who made B detective movies but was better known for his affair with Édith Piaf, was jealous of John spending so much time with Johnny, so I'd engage Eddie in conversation to let him know he wasn't playing second fiddle.

John let me make small decisions, such as should the vegetarian mobster chop up his own veggies or would an underling do it? "*You* decide," he'd say as he went off to talk to the cameraman. It made me feel important, and no one whispered behind my back that I was the director's *petite amie* or mistress. I was his creative assistant. In a few months, the film would be finished, and maybe I'd even see my name rolling down the credits as *directeur adjoint*, assistant director.

Most of the time, I'd stand next to John with a notepad. Once, he was going over a tracking shot with the cinematographer, but he didn't like the opening. He told the cameraman to put a plant on the edge of the frame, then turned to me and said, "I'd kill to have James Wong Howe here right now." Howe was the cameraman John had used on *He Ran All the Way*. "If the camera is going to track," John said, "it has to start somewhere and then reveal the action. James Wong Howe was brilliant with those details. He was one of the first cameramen to keep both the foreground and background in focus at the same time."

It was like having a private film mentor. Yes, Vincent had taught me how to eat snails and not to put ketchup on my oysters, but anyone could have taught me those things. John was educating me in what I hoped would be my new career: filmmaker.

One Sunday night, he said we were going over to James Jones's house for dinner. *That* James Jones, the author of *From Here to Eternity*. Jones owned a magnificent three-story house on the Isle St. Louis, and every other Sunday night, he and his wife, Gloria, would host spaghetti dinners for friends. The only reason we hadn't gone before was because John was so busy filming. I was afraid they'd look at John and think, *What are you doing with this girl younger than your daughter?*

The room was filled with American expat artists, musicians, and writers. I was introduced to William Styron and had no idea what to say to him. A Black man, Alex Haley, told everyone he was writing a book, and for the next thirty minutes, proceeded to talk out the plot of his story. I knew if he kept talking it, he'd never write it. Eyes were rolling in boredom, but Haley kept babbling on. The book we thought he'd never write became a best seller and TV series, *Roots*.

I was seated at dinner with John on one side and Jim on the other. They talked about John's movie as well as the book Jim was working on, *Go to the Widow-Maker*. Jim turned to me and asked, "Did you see *Masculin Féminin*?" Fortunately, John and I had seen the Godard film two nights ago, a film so tedious and the main actor talking so long I almost fell asleep; but it was *La Nouvelle Vague*, New Wave, and I wasn't about to criticize something I didn't understand.

I finally said, "I loved that the Jean-Pierre Léaud character called himself the child of Marx and Coca-Cola." One of the few lines I remembered. John was grinning and looking at Jim as if to say, *Isn't she bright?* And Jim gave John an *I'm impressed* look.

And then John said, "Margie is really a great writer."

I could feel myself blushing. When John and I had first started working on the script, I'd written my mother and told her I was falling in love with a brilliant blacklisted American film director. She'd answered, "Isn't he a little old for you, dear?" I wrote back and told her how his good friends had been Dalton Trumbo and Ring Lardner Jr., and that he'd been making a film about the Hollywood Ten when he was blacklisted and had to disappear or go to jail. Now he was writing and directing a new movie called, *À Tout Casser*.

My mother wrote back that she was very happy for me even if he was so much older, and did I know the *Daily Worker* had fired her because she panned a Communist film? She'd told me that story a hundred times. I wrote back that John was working with the hottest movie star in Paris, that people came to our apartment to interview him, and I was in love. She wrote back that she was so happy for me and looked forward to meeting him one day.

On the third of May 1968, there were suddenly police sirens everywhere as students protested against capitalism and consumerism. The students built barricades and threw paving stones and

Molotov cocktails at the police, who responded with tear gas. The French trade unions called for sympathy strikes, which quickly spread to more than eleven million workers protesting with the students. I begged John to go to the barricades, but he refused, saying it was much too dangerous. He was right, especially when photo after photo appeared in the French newspapers of bloodied students and policemen smashing students with their batons. It was the largest general strike ever in France, led by a German student leader, Daniel Cohn-Bendit, known as Dany le Rouge.

Everything was shut down, including John's movie and every other film in production. The filmmakers called for a general protest march, and John allowed us to go because he knew the police would never attack the famous moviemakers. There we were—John and me in the front row of marchers with Alain Resnais, Claude Chabrol, and Jean-Luc Godard. A photo of us in the front row made it into one of the French newspapers.

When we went to James Jones's house that Sunday night, John was the expert on the events, not only because he'd been a Communist, but because neither Jim nor his wife spoke enough French to understand what was happening. But what *was* happening? This was nothing like American protests I'd seen on TV about the Vietnam War or the civil rights demonstrations. Day after day, there were thousands of people in the streets. For weeks, every newspaper's front page showed confrontations between the protestors and the cops. We could walk around some neighborhoods of Paris, but we had to avoid those with barricades and violence. Everywhere, students and workers marched and shouted, "CRS . . . SS!" (CRS meaning *Compagnies Républicaines de Sécurité*, and SS meaning *Schutzstaffel*, Hitler's elite guard).

Six weeks went by. Paris was shut down. John tweaked the script. I'd go into the other room to work on my novel about a girl who goes to Paris and, unlike me, has many lovers.

One Sunday morning, John said, "Guess what we're doing today?"

"What?"

"We're going to Gladys's for brunch."

"Are you joking?" He'd barely mentioned his ex-wife in the two months we'd been living together.

"She wants to meet you. And I want you to meet the kids. They'll be there too."

Meeting his ex-wife and children? What exactly did this mean? Was he going to get their approval and then propose to me?

13

The Big Change in John

John and I pulled into the driveway of a large white house with green trim, his ex-wife's home in the Paris suburb of Sèvres. I checked to make sure there was no lipstick on my teeth.

John laughed. "What are you so nervous about?"

"I'm not nervous," I lied. How could I not be afraid to meet his ex-wife and two grown children?

A short woman with red hair and translucent skin smiled as she opened the door. "Hello, I'm Gladys. How nice to finally meet you." She kissed both my cheeks, as the French do. "Please come in." A younger version of John with the same thick, curly dark hair and pouty lips introduced himself: Denny, who was a year younger than me. Jan, a year older than me, bounced in from the kitchen and said hello.

We sat at a wooden table and Gladys served roasted chicken

and a pot of brown rice. John talked about his movie and Denny told John about the student film he was making. Jan stayed quiet.

"So, how do you like the chicken?" Gladys asked.

"This is the best chicken I've ever had." I meant it.

Gladys beamed. "It's corn-fed. See how yellow it is? That's what I want to talk to you about. John needs to eat healthy foods like chicken and macrobiotic brown rice. I'll write down the address of a butcher where you can buy corn-fed chickens. And every three to four months, it would be good if you could put him on the macrobiotic diet."

"The macrobiotic diet? Like Weight Watchers?"

"No, this is a ten-day diet that cleanses the body of toxins." She handed me three sheets of typed notes. "I wrote it up for you."

I glanced at the first page. It read, *MENU: follow scrupulously. Breakfast, lunch, and dinner: brown macrobiotic rice. Dinner every third night: add vegetables.*

"Rice for breakfast?"

She tried to reassure me. "It's very easy. This is an abridged version because a true macrobiotic diet would be only organic brown rice, but this works, and he always looks better after. Oh yes, and no coffee, but there's a beverage called Pero he can have as a substitute. After the ten days, you can switch to organic chicken with brown rice. You should try it, too, dear. You'll have so much energy, and you'll shine like an apple. It's very good to cleanse your body every three months." Now I understood what this get-together was about.

John and I tried the ten-day diet. The first three days were miserable, and we were starving. The coffee substitute, Pero, tasted like dirty dishwater. Our only look-forward-to was the steamed vegetables. But by the fourth day, we had boundless energy, and by day ten, we were glowing. John looked ten years younger, and I'd lost eight pounds. It wasn't as though I was fat before, but now, when I walked down the street and saw the slighter version of me in store windows, I felt a new confidence.

The Days of May were finally over, Paris was back to normal, and the film shoot was finished. John spent every day in the editing room. I was happy to stay home and work on my novel. Helping John write the script had given me confidence as a writer and taught me I could be funny. Each day, I'd invent new scenes inspired by my morning joint. I loved the ritual of pricking a needle into the hash cube, crumpling the heated softness into the weed, rolling it, and taking a huge inhale. I'd work for five hours straight before I got up from my chair.

When John returned from the editing room, we'd go out to a restaurant or to friends' homes for dinner. The French wives made everything by hand, even applesauce; they peeled, boiled, mashed, sliced, diced, and mixed. They pan-fried lamb in Calvados and *crème fraiche*. Watching them, I became proficient enough to serve dinner to our friends. I had to smile, remembering my mother had only cooked boiled hot dogs, Spam, and the chicken baked in Campbell's Tomato Soup.

One night, John's son Denny came to dinner with his new girlfriend, Jean Seberg, who was two years older than me. Jean was an American movie star who'd moved to Paris and starred in many French New Wave films, including *Breathless* with Jean-Paul Belmondo. I liked Jean but was jealous of Denny, whom she'd taken to New York City on a buying spree and bought him ten pairs of cowboy boots in every design and color.

Denny could have anything he wanted because Jean was rich.

It was different for us. When John had money, we lived like royalty, but his wealth waxed and waned with every movie—or lack of one. When he was flush, he'd lend hundreds of dollars to his fellow blacklisted expats. When broke, he'd borrow from them. Nothing was ever a loan, and no one ever expected to be paid back.

Jean and I became good friends. She told me how, when she lived in America, J. Edgar Hoover ordered the FBI to target her because she supported the Black Panthers. They planted false rumors saying she was having a child with a Black Panther member. Jean was so traumatized by the FBI's surveillance that she had a miscarriage in 1970. She also had an eight-year-old son, Diego, by her previous marriage to Romain Gary, a famous French novelist. Romain Gary lived in an apartment separated from Jean by a courtyard. Diego and I would hit a tennis ball against a brick wall. *"Tiens!"* Diego would say. *"Grand mère joue au tennis."* Look! Grandmother plays tennis. Considering I was twenty-six years old, it was hysterical to be called grandmother.

Jean also owned a beautiful home in Mallorca, and John and I joined them for vacation. Each morning, I'd wake up with the sunrise and take the narrow goat path down the hill while listening to the clinking goat bells and bird calls. I'd sit at an outdoor café overlooking the harbor, sip espresso, and watch the fishermen unload their catch. Now, fifty-five years later, whenever I try to meditate, I close my eyes and think of that serene walk down the goat path.

When we returned to Paris, John went back to the editing room, and I continued on my novel. I was completely in love. Even sewing a button on John's coat made me happy. I would have sat at his knees had he asked. And everything was perfect, until the day John entered the apartment looking so distraught, I thought something awful must have happened to Gladys or one of the kids.

"What's the matter, sweetie?" I moved toward him.

He turned away. "Goddamned cocksucker, motherfucker bastard."

"Who?" I asked.

"Kirschner." Kirschner was the French producer who *loved* John. We'd had dinner with him often.

"What happened?" I asked.

"He doesn't like my ending."

"Why not?"

"WHO THE FUCK KNOWS WHY NOT?"

I'd never heard John so angry. "What does he want you to do?"

"Nothing," he said. "He's already done it."

"Done what?"

"Pulled the film from me. COCKSUCKER! WHAT HAPPENED TO *LES DROITS D'AUTEUR*? In France, the rights always belong to the author, the creator of the film." John smashed his fist on the table. "Bastard!"

I winced. My father had smashed his hand down hard on the table every time he was fired. "HE'S NOT GOING TO GET AWAY WITH IT," John snarled. "I'll get every fucking French filmmaker in Paris to sign a petition. Truffaut. Godard. Rohmer. Renais. Chabrol. They'll all back me. NO ONE FUCKS WITH *LES DROITS D'AUTEUR*, GODDAMN IT." He pounded the table again. I backed away. Would he try to hit me the way my father had? For a second, I thought about leaving him, but he was fighting for his rights as an artist. I *had* to support him, because he'd win and go back to being his old self.

The following day, John returned to the producer's office. The doorbell rang. It was my sister Lynne, whom I hadn't seen in the three years since I'd left New York. She stood there with a suitcase. Lynne had never sent me a letter saying she was coming, and I knew she couldn't stay here, because it would be humiliating when she saw John out of control. I explained she couldn't stay, but didn't explain why, because I was so embarrassed.

I watched from the window as she lugged her heavy suitcase to the street. I wanted to call her back, but couldn't. What if she stayed, saw John in his rage, and told my mother? This happened fifty-five years ago, but I still can't believe I let my sister walk out into a city whose language she didn't speak, with no idea of where she'd go. It was the worst thing I ever did to her, and it haunts me to this day.

As he fought for the final cut, John's moods became worse. No matter how much the French purportedly respected authors' rights, John was losing the battle. He was going to take it to court, but the case wouldn't be heard for at least three months. Fortunately, around that time, John was offered a job at Circle in the Square directing *Boesman and Lena*, an off-Broadway play by South Africa's most famous playwright, Athol Fugard. The play would star James Earl Jones and Ruby Dee.

The timing was perfect because the owner of our sublet was coming back, and we'd have to leave anyway. When we flew to New York, I thought we'd return to Paris and find a new apartment, but secretly I knew this might be the end of our life there. At least we were returning to where I knew the language perfectly, because even though I spoke French fairly fluently, I'd always be an outsider. Too many times I'd smiled and pretended to understand what people were saying when I had no idea.

It was 1969. We found a small studio sublet on Tenth Street and University Place. My mother, grandmother, and Lynne all met John for the first time.

My mother said, "He's much too old for you."

Lynne said, "How can you make love with someone that old?"

My grandmother said, "Dearie, you can do better than that."

I was having my doubts, not because of anything they said, but because I'd now seen John's volatile side and was terrified he might hit me someday. Fortunately, the Athol Fugard play was a huge success, and John won an Obie Award as Best Director. Now, everyone in my family approved of him, but that also came with a downside. My grandmother, knowing John was my mother's age, said, "Surely John must know someone he could fix up with your mother?" I cringed.

In the theatrical world, success doesn't necessarily breed success. Even after *Boesman and Lena* opened to rave reviews, the phone didn't ring, which meant John wasn't contributing any income and had to ask his friends for handouts. Our rent was almost three hundred dollars a month. Miraculously, my mother found us a perfect, rent-stabilized Greenwich Village apartment for $158.36 a month, so at least *that* pressure was gone. The bad news was that life with John had become a roller-coaster ride.

During rehearsals of *Boesman and Lena*, I'd been both his creative assistant and the costume designer. Now that the play had opened and our jobs were finished, my new profession was being his secretary/nanny/cook/maid, and mistress. I barely had time to work on my novel.

He called his agent repeatedly, trying to drum up a new project. Nothing. And the longer he went without work, the nastier he became. There was no one else he could take it out on except me, but more and more, I wished I could find a way to be on my own. Finally, after months of no work when I'd just about given up and was thinking of leaving him, he received a call to direct James Earl Jones and Jill Clayburgh in *Othello* at the Mark Taper Forum in Los Angeles.

On the way to LA, we stopped off in Juárez, Mexico. It was coincidentally the last day for legal divorces. We'd spoken in the past about marriage, but he'd never formally proposed. And yes, as crazy as it sounds, I knew there was only one way I could get rid of him—marry him. Now that he'd won an Obie, my mother and grandmother no longer cared about the age difference. They encouraged me to marry him. I'd never told them about his abusive side.

John was at the courthouse getting his divorce, and I was in the Juárez hotel room about to wash my hair when the phone rang. "Come quickly!" John said. "The judge said he'd marry us. Hurry! He's about to leave for the day."

I jumped into a taxi, knowing if I married him, my mother and grandmother would finally stop nagging me. And as soon as the play in Los Angeles was over, I'd divorce him.

It wasn't how I envisioned my marriage. The judge spoke no English, so the ceremony was entirely in Spanish, and I have no idea what either of us promised. There was no wedding dress, no flowers. The receptionist handed me a dusty plastic lily from a vase. There was no ring, and I knew John didn't have money to buy one, but back home in my jewelry box was my grandmother's solid gold wedding band inscribed with her and her husband's initials and the date, *April 1911*. When we returned home, I'd wear that.

We flew from Juárez to Los Angeles and checked into the Biltmore. That night should have been a premonition of my rocky marriage, because at 4 a.m. I woke up to the sound of the TV and nightstand lamps crashing to the floor. The bed was rocking.

"Holy shit," said John, "it's an earthquake."

We threw on clothes, ran down the fifteen flights of stairs, and went outside with the other guests. There were huge cracks in the street. Half an hour later, the lobby had been swept clean of broken glass. Even the elevator worked.

But the *Othello* rehearsals were a new kind of earthquake. John was fighting with everyone except James Earl Jones. I didn't know if he was having a breakdown or if he was just so wounded from his experience with the French film that he couldn't concentrate. He decided the bed in which Othello kills Desdemona should be a mechanical masterpiece that would morph from a Venice dwelling into an archway, then into a bed. The device cost the production ten thousand dollars, but John insisted he needed it to make the play work. Because he'd so recently won an Obie, the producer agreed. But the bed never worked properly, and on opening night, it got stuck. The critics panned the play.

We returned to New York City. John sat around the apartment waiting for the phone to ring. It didn't. I was having a difficult time writing because he kept pacing back and forth, and the wooden floors creaked. One day, he was in horrible pain—a hernia. He checked into a hospital, where he was supposed to stay three nights. I was so happy being alone, not having to worry about his rages. The hospital called about his insurance. It seemed he'd lied and had none, so they kicked him out the next day. I couldn't have been more disappointed.

A few weeks later, we took Lynne to the Russian Tea Room for her birthday. I don't know what I said, but John suddenly lashed out at me and said, "You're crazy." Lynne looked at me in shock. After that night, his go-to phrase was calling me crazy. Was he worried I'd walk out? I would have, if I hadn't been so afraid of being alone.

His uncontrolled rages got worse. Once, he smashed his hand into the wall so hard, he made a hole in the plaster. Another night, I was heating up wonton soup, trying to persuade him to call his agent. He banged a chair against the floor and spit out, "You cunt, you're just like the rest of them." Then he flung the hot saucepan across the room, and the soup splattered all over the wall. I was terrified.

That night, I refused to sleep in the same bed as him. I slept on the couch. In a dream, my father came to me and said, "Get rid of him. He's not good enough for you." I woke up shaking. I'd never dreamed about my father before, so this had to be a warning. Wouldn't it be better to be alone than continue to bear the brunt of his fury? The next morning, I worked up the courage and told him I wanted a divorce.

"You cunt," he screamed. "Yeah, be a rat and desert the sinking ship." He banged his hand down hard on the table. I flinched and moved away from him. Finally, he packed up his clothes, threw his keys on the table, and thumped his suitcase down the five flights. I sat there shaking.

14

Life on My Own

My mother was not happy when I told her I'd left him. "Is it about a job?" she asked. "He'll get a job. Don't divorce him."

"It doesn't have anything to do with a job," I said.

"Then what is it?" she asked.

"You get married and suddenly you don't belong to yourself anymore."

"What are you talking about?" she said.

I didn't want to tell her about John's rages, so I said, "Look, all the wives who had kids never had their own career. I don't want to blame John if I don't do anything with my life, but it will be my fault if all I am is his wife."

"But Margie, there's nothing else out there," she argued. "Do you want to be all alone?"

"I don't want to be one of those people who holds on waiting for something that might never come. I have to go after it," I said.

Nothing she said could persuade me to take him back.

My grandmother called. "Don't you understand, dearie? There's nothing out there except love."

Despite their pleading, I had my marriage annulled. And, as strange and unlikely as it sounds, the week after I was in court, I was back at the same courtroom with the same judge to witness my sister's identical annulment.

Lynne and I went back to my apartment and got stoned. I was twenty-eight, she was twenty-six, and for the first time ever, we bonded. We laughed about how great our marriages had started out and how horribly they'd ended. We shared stories about our insane family. It was great until she left, and then everything felt hopeless. Who was I without John? I was a failure. I finally understood my father's depression. He'd failed at his job; I'd failed in marriage. I thought about jumping out the window, but I lived on the fifth floor, probably not high enough to guarantee death. And besides, I could never jump the way my father had. I had no gun, so that was out, too, and knowing me, I'd miss and end up still alive. Same with pills; death wasn't guaranteed. I could never slit my wrists, because it seemed too gruesome. I was much too afraid to consider any of those choices. I was stuck. I could wallow in my misery or try to do something about it.

The *Village Voice* had a job listing for an assistant at Grove Press, the publishing house of Ionesco, Beckett, Kerouac, Burroughs, and Allen Ginsberg. I landed the job, which turned out to be a secretarial job, but I didn't care because I was making money and working for the coolest publisher in town. My boss, Fred Jordan, was the nicest person I'd ever met, and even though I occasionally spelled his name "Jorden," he never got angry, just asked me to please spell it correctly the next time.

A few months later, I finished my novel, *Screw-Up*, and sent it off to eighteen agents. They all rejected it. Then, I remembered an agent who'd been a friend of my parents in Rowayton, Connecticut.

I sent it to him, and not much later, he sold the book to Berkley Press with a three-thousand-dollar advance. The book sold forty thousand copies, which I thought was huge, but it had taken two years to write and another year to get published, and three thousand dollars wouldn't last forever.

I wouldn't be quitting my job any time soon to write a new book, but now I had enough money to join the posh club Tennisport. Every night after work, I'd take the subway to Queens and play singles for two hours, and because many of the guys I played with were single, it was an easy way to meet men.

One evening, a date from Tennisport came to my apartment for drinks. He pulled out a small plastic bag of white powder, poured it onto a mirror, chopped it with a straight-edge razor, rolled up a dollar bill, and told me to inhale. It burned my nostrils, but after a couple of minutes, I no longer felt that deep, sorrowful pit in my stomach I'd been feeling since the divorce. I actually felt euphoric. I asked what it was, and he said cocaine.

From that moment on, cocaine became part of my life. You couldn't smell it like weed or alcohol, and you didn't slur your words. The more I used it, the less lonely and depressed I felt. One night, I decided to try to get into Studio 54. Normally, I would have been much too afraid to go by myself, but the cocaine made me feel invincible. A huge line waited around the block, but when the bouncer saw me in my silver jacket and long blond hair, he waved me in. I danced beneath the glittering coke spoon disco ball for hours, sometimes with partners, sometimes by myself. The coke gave me such confidence.

My go-to place to dance was the Lone Star Café on Thirteenth Street and Fifth Avenue with a giant iguana sculpture on the roof. That's where I first heard Dr. John, whom they introduced as Mac Rebennack. One night, Doug Sahm of the Sir Douglas Quintet, who wrote *Mendocino*, was playing there, and I was dancing by myself near the stage. When the band took a break, Doug Sahm introduced himself and invited me back to the Grammercy Hotel. We went back to his room and did coke.

The great thing about cocaine was that when I was high, all these incredible ideas would come to me, and I'd race to my typewriter to get the thoughts down. Unfortunately, when I read them back the next morning, it was complete gobbledygook. Not one sentence made sense.

In the meantime, my job at Grove Press suddenly became very exciting, because they created a Grove Press International Film Festival with screenwriters and directors from around the world. Because I spoke French, I was selected to pick up the talent from the airport, escort them to their hotel, and translate their answers for the journalists. I never understood half of what they said in French, but I figured out enough words to creatively make up sentences. Fortunately, no one ever questioned my translations.

When the festival ended, it was back to typing letters. Time to find a new job. There was an ad in *Backstage* for an office manager at a commercial film production company. The owner sat me down and asked me my long-term goals. I told him I wanted to write and direct films.

"You don't want to be an office manager," he said. "An office manager sits behind a desk. If you want to direct, you have to learn how to edit first." He suggested I call Morty Fallick, who edited commercials. "Tell him you heard he was the best editor in New York, and you want to work for him. Tell him he won't have to pay you until you're more valuable to him than he is to you." It was the best advice anyone ever gave me—actually, it was the only advice anyone had *ever* given me.

Morty Fallick hired me. How could he not? I was working for free! I learned how to synch 16mm and 35mm film, cut the outtakes with a razor-sharp guillotine, splice the new cut together with mylar, thread the Moviola, and play the new cut. I loved my job, and after only four months, Morty started paying me.

The only thing I hated were the Madison Avenue agency clients he had to deal with. The big shots stood behind Morty and haggled with each other whether a scene should be two frames shorter or one frame longer. Did a pipe sitting on the table look as though the husband had died? Their suggestions were ridiculous, but Morty sat there hour after hour until finally they were back to the cut he had suggested in the first place.

Six months after I started working there, Morty was hired to direct a documentary film on the Holy Shroud of Turin. On the linen shroud, purportedly found after Christ's crucifixion, was an image of a body whose head had been covered in a thorny crown and whose back showed the scourge marks of someone who had been horribly beaten.

The film was to be shot in Europe and would trace the Holy Shroud's journey from France to England. Morty would interview experts along the way. The final location would be the Cathedral of Turin in Italy, where the Holy Shroud is kept in three locked boxes. Because some of the shooting would be in France, I was hired as French translator, script girl, photographer, and assistant director.

The shoot was an extraordinary experience and, even better, when we returned to NYC, I wrote the script, hired and directed James Earl Jones as the narrator, and edited the film, which won an Emmy Award for best documentary. Unfortunately, making *The Holy Shroud of Turin* had been a lucky fluke, because soon I was back to synching dailies and listening to the ad agency clients bicker with Morty. This was not for me. I put out feelers and learned of a job for a writer at a company called PCS (Planned Communication Services) that made public service announcements (PSAs), video news releases (VNRs), and marketing films.

They made me write a sample PSA, and I landed the job. It didn't take long before I was not only writing the scripts but directing and producing as well. The job paid what I thought was a fortune (forty thousand a year), and I could hire the crew and supervise the editor. During good weather, I'd shoot in the city, but in winter we needed exteriors, so I'd fly to Los Angeles and stay at the Beverly Hills Hotel on the company's dime. I felt like a big shot, and I was doing what I loved.

One of the company's clients was ASTA (American Society of

Travel Agents), whose yearly conference concluded with a Travel Hall of Fame film, honoring those who'd contributed the most to travel in the twentieth century. I'd interview and film the winners, write the script, and create three-minute filmographies. As there was always a winner from Europe or Asia, I traveled first class on Pan Am to Ireland, Thailand, Japan, and India. This was long before video production, and it took weeks to get the final film print back from the color lab. As a result, I had to hand-deliver the film to wherever the conference was being held, which could be the Philippines, or Madrid, or Montreal, or any place in the world.

Besides delivering the print, my job was to debrief the MC who'd introduce the film. One year, the conference was in Rio. Mayor John Lindsey was the MC, and I couldn't get hold of him to explain his role. I saw him jogging on the beach, so I chased him down. A photo of us running made the front page of the top Brazilian newspaper.

My films received many awards, including the most coveted prize in advertising, the ANDY Award. For a PSA on hand tool safety, I filmed actor/prisoners trying to break out of jail using hand tools, then being caught by the guard, who made them put their tools away. As I walked up to the stage to receive my award, I couldn't stop grinning. I was *not* the nobody my parents thought I was, and I was *not* the crazy person John claimed. I'd done this all on my own.

I continued to make films, play tennis, and snort cocaine. I'd now been at PCS five years and loved my job, but my salary was still forty thousand. As I'd won so many awards, I asked for a raise. My boss said creativity didn't pay and that the purpose of this company was to book and ship. The only way I'd make more money, he said, was to work on commission. I had no intention of doing that and told him so. Then he relented and offered me an expense account of seventy-five dollars a week.

Now I could rent a car every summer weekend and go upstate to a little cabin on the Ashokan Reservoir, where I was the "security guard." My job was to give out one-dollar tickets to anyone who wanted to paddle a canoe to the other side. One day while driving to Ashokan, I heard Flatt and Scruggs on the radio and decided to take up banjo. I found a five-string for twenty dollars, sat outside my cabin, and plucked away, playing so badly even the chipmunks ran away. A few weeks later, I sold the banjo. I needed to find an easier instrument to play.

One winter day in the mid-1970s, I noticed an ad in *Rolling Stone*: "Learn to Play Blues Harmonica: $7.95 with a free harmonica." The package arrived, but I couldn't understand the instructions. I noticed that the author lived in San Diego, where I was heading in a few weeks to film. I found his phone number, called him long distance, and arranged to take a harmonica lesson in person. He taught me a little riff, and once I arrived back home, I practiced but soon got bored, so I threw away the instrument. I mention this because thirty-five years later, the harmonica would again become part of my life.

On another trip, my flight from San Francisco to Los Angeles was delayed, and I sat waiting. A guy about ten years older than me, carrying a huge boom box, approached and asked in a Southern drawl, "Do you like music?"

"Of course," I said. He introduced himself as Bob Johnston, handed me headphones, and said, "Listen to this." His eyes smiled. I'd never seen anyone radiate so much energy.

"That's Joe Ely," he said. "I'm producing him."

I'd never heard of Joe Ely, but I loved the song. As our flight continued to be delayed, we talked. Bob Johnston was a record producer and had produced Bob Dylan's *Highway 61 Revisited* and *Blonde on Blonde*, Johnny Cash's *At Folsom Prison*, Simon and Garfunkel's *Parsley, Sage, Rosemary and Thyme*, plus albums of Aretha Franklin and Leonard Cohen.

It turned out he traveled back and forth from Mill Valley to LA and New York almost as often as I traveled the world. We reconnected whenever we were in the same city, but he was completely irresponsible. He'd say he'd meet me at 6 p.m. and show up at 9 p.m., but he was mesmerizing and always had new music to share. He invited me to some recording sessions, including one with Jimmy Cliff at Electric Lady in NYC. Cliff was so stored he could barely sing. Sometime during the session, Bob Dylan called to ask if Johnston could produce him immediately, but unfortunately, Bob was stuck with a super-stoned Jimmy Cliff and had to turn down Dylan's request. It was the only time I ever saw him furious.

Once, Bob was producing John Mayall in LA, years before Mayall's house burned down in Laurel Canyon. I knew nothing about the blues and had no idea who John Mayall was, but I got to know him from the recording session and was invited to a few of his wild parties. I never dared jump from the second floor into the pool as others did. And I didn't learn much about music, but plenty about networking. I needed two kids for a PSA I was shooting in a few days and John's son, Jason, hooked me up with Moon Unit and Dweezil, Frank Zappa's kids. I didn't meet Zappa, but his kids were in my film.

It was now my tenth year at PCS. One day, my boss called me into his office and said his children were grown and his wife needed a career. He wanted me to train her to become a director/producer. I could see where this was going—he obviously wanted to take his wife to the wonderful places where we shot, but there was no reason for her to be there unless she was part of the crew. I took her on a few local shoots, but she was clueless, and I knew she'd never make it as a director.

Soon after, my boss said I'd be going to New Orleans to shoot a PSA while he and his wife were headed to Switzerland, where his wife would direct a marketing film for a hotel chain. *WHAT?* I had a feeling my days were numbered, but I didn't want to quit because I'd never find such a great job. And then, out of the blue, I received a phone call that would not only change my life, but turn me into a Cinderella who never had to leave the ball.

15

Outward Bound Changes My Life

Out of the blue, an old friend called, telling me he was on the board of Outward Bound and asking if I'd like to join an adult invitational river-rafting trip—five days paddling Lodore Canyon on the Green River in Utah. I'd never been on a rafting trip or slept in a sleeping bag, but the more he told me about it, the more it sounded like Girl Scout camp without cookies. I said no, but he was persistent. He described the scenery: vermillion-colored canyon walls rising 2,500 feet above the river, and gentle rapids to run, not scary ones. I accepted.

Sixteen of us met at the river, blew up the rafts, and were assigned a partner to share a waterproof dunnage bag. I was surprised I was assigned a guy, but when we loaded our stuff and Howard dragged the bag to the raft, I understood. The gear bag was heavy, and as neither of us wanted to be far away from our belongings, we slept next to each other under a universe of stars. We talked deep into the night, and I learned Howard was married, had two kids, lived in Scarsdale, and had a hedge fund.

"Are you a gardener?" I asked.

After he stopped laughing, he explained he managed a pool of money from many investors. I told him I had a film-production company, was divorced, and loved tennis. He said he knew someone I might like, a divorced corporate lawyer who was a spectacular tennis player. I said I'd meet him, but he had to beat me in tennis.

The next day, we docked the rafts near a gigantic rock cliff. "We're going to belay," the instructor said. "You will each have a chance to climb up the cliff, roped in. An instructor will be up top, so if you fall, you won't fall more than five feet." As I looked up at the cliff, which looked taller than the Empire State Building, a corporate titan as big as a football player volunteered to go first. It seemed to take him forever to get up the rock, and at one point, I heard him let out a sob. I moved to the very back of the line.

One by one, we ascended to the top. It was my turn, and I was terrified. The instructor hooked my harness to the rope and said, "Remember, find the finger holes in the rock and use your legs to pull you up."

I looked for a place to start. My mouth was so dry I could barely swallow. As instructed, I called out, "On belay," then put one foot on the rock. There was no perch for my other foot and no crack to grab with my hands. Three times I tried but couldn't find a hold. I wanted to quit, but the Outward Bound motto is "To Serve, To Strive, and Not to Yield." I would not yield, no matter what. My foot finally found a ledge, my finger found a crevice, and I was climbing. Step by step, hand over hand. It was easy. And then, just like that, I was at the top of the rock face.

"Holy cow!" the instructor said. "You're Spider-Woman."

I couldn't stop grinning. I'd achieved something impossible and knew if I could climb this scary rock face, I could do anything

At lunch that day, I sat next to Dave, who told me he was head of marketing at AT&T. He asked what I did, and I told him I wrote, produced, and directed public service announcements and marketing films. I could see he was interested, but I didn't try to sell, not even when he asked what two sixty-second PSAs would cost. I said twenty thousand each, knowing my company would profit thirty thousand for the two. Then, I thought, if my boss's wife is going to replace me, why let them have all this profit? I would quit my job and start my own company with AT&T as my first client.

As soon as I returned to New York, I called the lawyer who'd handled my divorce, quit my job, and two days later, created MG Productions. I found a small office sublet, hired my first employee, and produced the two PSAs for AT&T. But what if I never got another client? Fortunately, because I said AT&T was my client, I landed a second client, then a third, and soon MG Productions was rolling along. The best thing? I was my own boss. A friend who also had her own business said, "Welcome to the jungle."

A few weeks later, Howard, my Outward Bond dunnage partner, called. Did I want to meet his friend Jack, the divorced lawyer? I said yes, providing our first date was a tennis match. Jack came to the Village to pick me up. He had expressive eyes and a soothing voice. He reminded me of the euphorbia, a very attractive plant that, if you cut even slightly, a milky white poison drips out. The poison, for me, was that Jack was at least twenty pounds overweight. I'd never dated a heavy guy. I wondered how he could play tennis with all that weight, but he beat me 6-0, 6-0.

I liked him, but hated that he was fat. When we went to dinner, he must have read my mind, because he told me he was on a diet. And maybe he had extra pounds, but he was super smart and could talk about anything. We learned we both shared dysfunctional families. He was thrilled I'd published a novel and that I had my own production company. He thought it was cute that I lived in the Village in a fifth-floor walk-up and called me a Village Rat, but not disparagingly.

I don't think he'd ever been with a woman who wore jeans. He lived in a posh Midtown East rental with views of the East River from every room. His two children, fifteen and seventeen, lived with his ex-wife in Scarsdale. When I asked him what it was like to be a corporate lawyer, he said it was like being a psychiatrist to his heavy-hitter clients. How did he get clients, I asked. He called it rainmaking. "Just let them talk about themselves," he said.

He called the next day to ask me out, but I lied and told him I was busy. What if he really wasn't planning to lose weight? A day later, he called again. I asked how his diet was coming. He said he'd lost two pounds. I congratulated him, but continued to stall him, because anyone could lose two pounds. He kept calling. I always said I was busy, but always asked how his diet was coming.

Meanwhile, I continued to get new business, and whenever I bid against my old company and won, I was thrilled. I kept the expenses low by renting out film equipment, the editing room, and sound studio for each shoot. As potential clients often wanted to meet at my office, I sublet a huge office from a sleek design firm with access to a large conference room. My office was the first from the entrance, so it looked as though the entire space and the sixteen employees were all part of MG Productions. To add to the hype, I bought a phone system with ten extensions for production, editing, scheduling, distribution, etc. All the lines bounced back to my producer, but no one knew.

Whenever I won an award, I'd send a release to *The New York Times* and all the trade publications. More work flowed in. Jack continued to call, and I continued to say I was busy, though I always asked how his diet was coming. I really looked forward to his calls, and I think he knew exactly what was going on.

The Greater New York Salvation Army wanted me to make a public service announcement with Whitney Houston about helping children, and they wanted to shoot on St. Patrick's Day. I hired a studio, crew, lighting designer, teleprompter, and operator, and ordered green bagels and green roses. We arrived at the studio and waited, but no Whitney. Two hours went by. Finally, Whitney's assistant called to say that Whitney couldn't make it. No reason given. My heart sank. Fortunately, the entire shoot was insured.

We rescheduled for the following week, and this time Whitney showed. She couldn't have been nicer, but Robin, her assistant, kept scowling at me. When I brushed a strand of hair off Whitney's face, Robin swatted my hand away, and said, "Don't you dare touch her." Years later, I realized Whitney must have been too stoned to shoot the day she didn't show up, and that Robin obviously had a much bigger role than as Whitney's assistant.

Two months went by. Jack called and said he'd lost twenty pounds. I eagerly said yes to dinner. This might make me seem like a horribly superficial person, but I knew if we were going to become a couple—which I was sure we would—that I needed to feel good about putting my arms around him.

We went out three nights in a row, and Jack invited me to a formal black-and-white charity event. I explained I had no formal dress, so I couldn't go. "I'll take you to Bergdorf Goodman," he said. "I'll set up an appointment with a personal shopper."

"But I can't afford a dress from Bergdorf's," I said.

"Well, I'm paying," he said. "I invited you, so it's my responsibility."

"I can't let you pay," I said, and meant it. But he was persuasive, and that Saturday, we were escorted into a plushy private dressing room at Bergdorf's, where we sipped Tab, Coke's first diet soda. The personal shopper helped me into gown after luxurious gown. The one I liked best was a black Ungaro, which fit perfectly.

"That's the one," Jack said. I sneaked a peak at the price tag. It was three thousand dollars. I protested, but Jack was adamant. I told him it didn't feel right to spend that much money on a dress. He laughed and said, "Get used to it."

After the charity ball, where I felt exactly like Cinderella, we saw each other almost every night. We often ate at the Four Seasons Restaurant (no longer there), which Jack called his cafeteria. We'd also dine there with his clients, whose wives dressed in designer clothes, expensive jewelry, and glittery watches. I was stuck talking to them while the client held Jack's attention. It wouldn't have been so bad, but mostly they bragged about their children and not much else.

One night, Jack said he'd like to take me on a vacation to anywhere I wanted to go. I didn't have to think about it. He'd lost the weight but needed some toning, so I suggested Canyon Ranch, a health resort in Arizona where I'd always wanted to go but hadn't because it was so expensive. We flew first class and stayed in the best casita on the property. We'd start the morning on a desert hike, then I'd go to the high-energy aerobic classes, and he'd go to men's stretch, and we'd meet for meals. It was a perfect week; he lost the flab and looked great.

We were sitting in the Tucson airport lounge, waiting for our flight back to NYC, asking each other questions.

"What's the worst thing about you?" he asked.

"It's too embarrassing to tell you," I said.

"Were you a felon?" he asked.

"Of course not," I laughed, and then admitted I'd done a lot of drugs. He seemed relieved, so I didn't tell him I was still doing coke, and hadn't brought it with me only because I didn't want to get caught at the airport by some sniffing dog. Then Jack told me his Alpha Romeo Spider was getting old and asked what my dream car was. Mercedes?

"Oh no," I said. "I don't like touring cars. A yellow Porsche Cabriolet 911,"

A week later, Jack and I drove to the Manhattan Porsche dealership. There was no yellow Porsche, but there was a shiny red 911 Cabriolet, which he bought on the spot. We hadn't even been dating that long.

A few weeks later, we went down to his garage to get the car out on our way to play tennis. I was about to get in the passenger's side when Jack said, "You might want to look at the license plate."

It read, "4 Margie." Was this really happening to me?

Part III

16

The Good Life

Jack and I had been dating six months. He was forty-four and I was forty-two. My good friend Susan asked if we planned to get married, and I told her he hadn't proposed. When she insisted I find out, I told her I didn't know how. "Just ask him where this relationship is going," she said. It wasn't in my nature to say what I wanted, but Susan kept pressing. One night, Jack and I were having dinner, and I tried to bring up the subject, but couldn't. We finished dessert and he called for the check when I blurted out, "Um, where are we were going with this relationship?"

He squeezed my hand and smiled. "Wherever you want it to go."

Two weekends after that, we took the Porsche out for a spin, because a Porsche is like a horse and needs its head. The passenger's job was to get the toll token out of a case in the dash compartment. I was driving as we approached the toll booth.

"Jack," I said, "I need the token!"

"You might want to get it yourself," he said.

How could I downshift and steer and open the case all at the same time? I pulled the car to the side of the road, opened the case, and gasped. On top of the tokens was a two-carat diamond solitaire ring, exactly what I wanted, but about four times bigger than I could ever have imagined. Jack slipped the ring on my finger, and I watched the diamond glitter in the sunlight, envisioning a wedding where I wouldn't be holding a plastic lily in Mexico with no ring.

My mother and I looked at wedding venues—the Pierre, the St. Regis, and the Plaza. I liked the St. Regis best, and we sat with the wedding planner discussing the menu. I wanted to start with shrimp cocktail.

"But dear," my mother whispered, "that will cost more!"

I said nothing. I told the wedding planner we'd be 150 people.

"We'll need place settings for one hundred and fifty-one," my mother chimed in.

"Why?" I asked.

"Because my friend Rachel the photographer has to eat."

"*What?* She's there to shoot pictures, not be a wedding guest," I said. I knew this was only the beginning. My mother would drive me crazy, and I'd be miserable at my own wedding. There's no free lunch, not even in Cinderella Land. I was in tears when I told Jack.

"Don't worry" he said. "We'll do the wedding ourselves."

We narrowed the guest list down to seventeen people in the private room at Sign of the Dove, the most romantic restaurant in New York City. We hired what Jack jokingly called a rent-a-rabbi and exchanged vows in a corner of the room. Later, when I looked at the photos, I noticed we'd gotten married directly below an EXIT sign. That should have been a portent of the future, just as the LA earthquake had uprooted my honeymoon with John.

During the wedding toasts, Jack's fifteen-year-old son raised his glass and said, "May you have health, happiness, and no more kids." A few people gasped, but it didn't bother me because having children had never been my dream. I didn't want to give up my career or tennis or the ability to travel anywhere if we were burdened down by a child. Jack wouldn't have minded having another kid, and also said I didn't need to work and should give up my company. No way. My job gave me respect and self-worth.

I continued to work as a filmmaker during the day; evenings, I was a corporate wife attending endless dinners and charity events. Not just attending. Jack insisted I look the part, which meant dressing in designer clothes. When I'd filmed in India, I'd learned that a woman's jewelry is a clear indication of the husband's wealth. But the designer clothes Jack wanted me to wear were outrageously expensive. I'd try on a couture dress, and even though Jack had given me my own credit card, I just couldn't stomach the thought of paying three thousand dollars or more for an outfit. I'd return from Bergdorf's or Saks and tell him I couldn't do it. He'd say, "Do I have to go there with you?"

Finally, I gave in. I'd meet the personal shopper twice a month, then return home laden with Valentino, Lagerfeld, and Ungaro. If I didn't shop often enough, he'd tease me, "Isn't it time to go see Manny?" (His name for Emanuel Ungaro, my favorite designer.) Eventually, I understood this was part of the corporate wife lifestyle and gave in.

But I would not change my watch, no matter how many times Jack said I needed something more appropriate. I wore a twenty-dollar Snoopy Timex with a turquoise Zuni band I'd bought in Arizona. Jack took me to Tourneau to try on five-thousand-dollar Piaget and Cartier watches, but they were too glitzy for me. Every time we walked out empty-handed, he'd say, "Don't worry, I'll break you yet."

I wasn't a horse. He couldn't break me from my Snoopy watch, but I was thrilled he'd gotten me out of my fifth-floor rent-controlled walkup. I never minded the five flights, but there was no air conditioning, and the owner wouldn't allow us to wire because she wanted us out. In summer, the apartment was so unbearably hot I went to the Quad Cinema and sat in the cool theatre until the last movie ended. I would now joke to Jack that I married him for his air conditioning.

We moved into a three-bedroom apartment Midtown East with a perfect view of the East River. The second bedroom was in case one of his kids spent the night, and the third bedroom was my home office. One Saturday, I tried writing in the new office, but suddenly there was Jack, looking over my shoulder. I could never write with him around.

We lived a couple of blocks from the East River, so every morning we'd get up early and run three miles along the river path. After a few months, Jack found excuses not to run and was putting on the pounds again, probably from all the meals we ate out. I remained thin by doing cocaine but never told him about it, as there was no reason for him to know. Besides, not only would he be hooked like me, but I imagined a lawyer might be disbarred for doing drugs.

Everything was perfect, but there was just one hitch—after twenty-two years of remission and having cancer four times in the last fifty years, my mother developed bone cancer and was put in the hospital. One day, she pressed her call button for a bedpan, but no one answered, so she got out of bed and broke her hip. After three weeks, the hospital insisted she had to go home. Jack wrote a letter on his firm's letterhead threatening to sue if they tried to release her, as they were responsible for not answering her call button. After that, they stopped trying to release her.

My mother remained in the hospital week after week, then month after month. After seven months, she was begging to go home. The head nurse explained if she were to be released, I'd have to be the key giver, have a hospital bed installed, and make sure there were round-the-clock nurses, which I was responsible for finding. If a nurse didn't show, I'd have to race down to my mother's apartment.

What if I were out of town? I told her I couldn't be the key giver. I felt guilty about it, but knew it was better than being available 24/7 and resentful. So, every day after work, I'd take a taxi downtown to see her. And then I'd have to race back home, change, and go to a corporate client event with Jack. It was exhausting.

One day, the nurse called to say my mother had metastatic bone cancer, which would eventually spread to her lungs, but there was good news—the hospital had just built a brand-new hospice unit, and she'd be much more comfortable there. Wouldn't it make sense to move her? By the time I arrived at the hospital, my mother was in the new unit. She looked at me with one furious pale blue eye, because the other had begun to close.

"Do you know what hospice *means*?" she spit out.

I knew exactly what it meant, but I said, "It means they take really good care of you here, and this is much nicer than a regular hospital room."

"I want to go home," she said, crossing her bone-thin hands defiantly across her chest.

"I'm sorry, Mom. Believe me, they can take better care of you here."

A few weeks later, the nurse called saying my mother was about to go into a coma and I should come quickly, the end would be soon. I called my sister Lynne and raced to Beth Israel, where my mother lay slumped to one side. The nurse said she was in a coma but could still hear. I pulled up a chair to the side of the bed.

"Hi Mom," I said. There was no response.

I stared at the cheap watch on her frail wrist. If she didn't pass away today, I'd have to return yet again to pick up her watch, clothes, and toiletries. If we took everything now, we'd never have to come back here again. I could just reach down, unfasten the worn leather strap, and slip the watch off her wrist. Her watery pale blue eye was half open, and she seemed to be staring at me. I couldn't bring myself to remove the watch. Lynne wouldn't do it, either.

I looked at my mother's lopsided body, her back caved in from the cancer. So many months I'd been coming to the hospital. I detested the elevator that stopped on every floor. I hated the sickly smell that permeated the corridors, and walking by the nurses' station with vases of half-dead flowers and semi-deflated "Get Well" balloons. I didn't want to return here ever again.

I reached down to her wrist, but at that moment, she jerked her head slightly. I motioned to Lynne that we should empty out her closet. She'd come here in November, now it was May. All her wool clothes were on hangers. We grabbed a plastic bag and silently filled it with clothes, shoes, and her faded beige bra with the two mastectomy forms. How many years had she been wearing that heavy bra? Thirty? More?

It was hard to be resentful of someone who had endured so much pain. We emptied her bedside table of hand lotion, eyeglasses, and a small transistor radio. Then, I fumbled with her watch strap, finally slipping it off her stick-thin wrist. I clasped her lifeless hand and whispered, "Goodbye, Mom, I love you." It was the first time I'd said "I love you" to her since the day I'd left for Europe twenty years earlier. As soon as I got outside the hospital, I threw the watch and her clothes into a trash basket. I didn't cry.

The next morning, the nurse called to say my mother had died. "You have to come and identify her body and claim her things," she said.

"But I took everything yesterday!" I protested.

"There's a box with her name on it. They brought it to storage."

I couldn't bear to identify her body, but fortunately, my aunt volunteered. In the hospital's basement, I waited for the attendant to hand me a large cardboard box on which my mother's name had been written. Inside was a polka-dot dress, gray sweater, and a pair of brown shoes.

"These aren't my mother's things," I said angrily.

"I'm sorry," the attendant said. "It must have been mislabeled."

Later that day, Lynne and I went to my mother's apartment, cluttered with books, magazines, stacks of self-help tapes, New Age crystals, and incense sticks. We took a few pieces and threw away the rest—wigs left over from chemotherapy, drawers full of letters, and her diary in which she tried to will her cancer cells away. There was an old suitcase full of her writings dating back to the '40s. I began to read them—short stories about herself, beautifully written. But I was so angry with her for dying without telling me her wishes that I threw out the suitcase. It was the stupidest thing I've ever done.

That same night, Jack and I attended a charity event in which one of his most important clients was honored. As I sat at the event in my designer gown and sparkly jewelry, listening to boring speeches, I thought about my mother. She'd wanted to do some good in the world, but in the end she was stuck with many recurrences of cancer, a schizophrenic daughter, a husband who ended his life, and all her unfulfilled dreams. For years after, I was haunted by that pale blue eye squinting at me. She must have known I'd taken her watch, and making me feel guilty was her way of getting even. That night, right in the middle of the important client's speech, my tears began to flow.

17

Too Good to Be True

Life with Jack continued to be unreal. As if the huge diamond engagement ring, the sixteen-diamond wedding band, the Porsche and vanity license plate, and the Manhattan apartment with drop-dead East River views weren't enough, we bought a brand-new seven-thousand-square-foot all-glass weekend house on a private lane in Greenwich, Connecticut. I say "we," because Jack insisted we were co-owners even though he paid. There was a ground-floor master suite, four other bedrooms with private baths, a living room the size of a pickleball court, a dining room seating twelve, and an outdoor Jacuzzi spilling into a large, heated pool. In front of the house was a serene pond surrounded by forsythia trees. For our anniversary, we commissioned a fourteen-by-five-foot painting of the view from the front of the house.

Jack's firm had offices in Europe, so we went to Paris at least three times a year, eating in Michelin-starred restaurants and staying in the Penthouse suite of the Bristol Hotel, whose private terrace was larger than a basketball court. One morning, we were in our hotel bathrobes. He was reading something in the bed, and I sat at the vanity table spraying on the sweet floral and Oriental scent of *Paris* by Yves Saint Laurent, which I'd bought the day before. This was all too good to be true. I felt like a queen, especially knowing how I'd had nothing as a child—no vacations, no eating out, and lousy Spam or chicken doused with Campbell's Tomato Soup dinners at home. Here I was in the fanciest suite in Paris and living a life I never could have imagined.

Besides trips to Paris and vacations in Positano and Marrakesh and the south of France, we sometimes traveled to luxury resorts on his clients' private jets. A town car would drive onto the tarmac, and our suitcases would be whisked away. It wasn't just private jets. It was also private helicopters. Donald Trump was one of Jack's many outside lawyers, and in June 1988, we went with eight other people, including Jack Nicholson, on Trump's Sikorsky helicopter to Atlantic City. This was long before Trump was on *The Apprentice*. He'd invited us to watch the boxing match between Mike Tyson and Michael Spinks at the Taj Mahal, which at the time he owned. Stretch limos whisked us by police escort to the Taj, where we walked down the long-carpeted aisle toward the arena, Trump leading the way. People crowded in and tried to touch him, thinking that would lead to instant wealth.

Jack and I were at the wedding in 1993 when Marla married Trump. Their wedding venue was the Plaza (which he owned at the time), and guests included the Clintons, Simon Cowell, Billy Joel, and Barbara Walters. We watched Trump at the front of the room as he fidgeted and waited for Marla (who had given birth to their daughter, Tiffany, two months before) to walk down the aisle. After a good fifteen minutes that felt like five hours, Marla finally made her appearance.

Marla didn't come to the boxing match, but I was stuck there. I detest boxing because I hate violence (though I love boxing with my trainer, where I never get hurt). I tried to figure out how long thirteen rounds would take. An hour? More? Suddenly, there were huge cheers as Tyson and Spinks, both undefeated, slipped under the ropes and took off their robes to show off glistening muscled bodies. It was the most expensive fight in boxing history, grossing seventy million dollars. Almost immediately, Tyson knocked Spinks down. Spinks got up. Tyson punched again and this time knocked Spinks out. The fight lasted all of ninety-one seconds. For a minute, everyone was whispering, "It's fixed," but I was elated. It was over! We could go home.

I didn't tell anyone about our experience with Trump or the kind of life I led, because I wanted to be an ordinary person in my day-to-day life. Yet, as perfect as my life was, I was getting bored with the endless client dinners where Jack talked nonstop with the client and I was stuck making small talk with the wife. To make it bearable, every half hour I'd head to the ladies' room and snort coke.

There was one corporate CEO whose wife I really liked. She and her superstar CEO husband had a weekend mansion in Greenwich, and she and I would go for walks every Saturday morning.

"Don't get too close to her," Jack said, "because if her husband is fired, you won't be able to play with her anymore."

Was everything based on business? Another time, one of the wives wasn't getting along very well with her husband; a few months later, after thirty years of marriage and three children, he would leave her for a man. As we were eating, she whispered to me, "Buy as much jewelry as you can. It will always be worth a fortune and lasts a lot longer than a husband." But I didn't care about expensive jewelry and knew Jack and I would last forever.

One of Jack's partners was good friends with Hillary Clinton, and as Jack's firm had made a substantial donation to the campaign, we were invited to the White House along with twenty other VIP guests, one of whom took us to DC on his helicopter. Clinton himself gave us a tour of the Oval Office and the Lincoln bedroom and showed us the exact spot where Prime Minister Yitzhak Rabin of Israel and Palestinian leader Yasir Arafat signed the first Oslo accord. "I almost had to push Arafat to shake Rabin's hand," Clinton said. We were ushered into a room for cocktails, and waiters passed around drinks with the White House logo on paper napkins. I stuffed a few into my purse. Surprisingly, there were no hors d'oeuvres, just peanuts.

The guests included newlyweds Lyle Lovett and Julia Roberts, and while I'm a huge Lyle Lovett fan, I was much too intimidated to tell him how much I loved his music. Lovett is a Lincoln fan, so he and Julia spent as much time as they could ogling and canoodling in the Lincoln bedroom.

During cocktails, Hillary and Bill made the rounds separately, greeting us each individually. "Welcome, Jack and Margie," Bill said, putting his arm on my shoulder. *How did he know our names?* Then I saw an aide just behind him. Bill was absolutely charming and spent a great deal of time with us, as if we were his only guests. After he moved on to greet another couple, Hillary approached, also knowing our names.

I whispered, "I wish it had been you, not him." She gave me a little smile and said nothing, but I could tell she wished the same.

It was a once-in-a-lifetime experience, but even better was the invitation by the president of Loews Hotel to come to Monaco and watch the Dream Team play an exhibition game prior to the 1992 Barcelona Olympics. The hotel, meals, and watching the Dream Team practice and play the exhibition game were all comped.

Jack, a huge basketball fan, was still in shock when we arrived in Monaco, changed into our swimsuits, and went to the outdoor pool on the roof. Larry Byrd, all six foot nine of him, stood cradling his young baby. Magic Johnson, also six foot nine, lay on a recliner with his knees dangling over. The entire Dream Team was staying there, guests of Prince Rainier. We were walking in the hallway when Scottie Pippen, holding hands with his girlfriend, stopped us and asked if we knew the way to the beach.

After lunch, we watched the Dream Team scrimmage against

each other. Here we were, just a few people in a stadium that seats 18,500, feet away from the most famous basketball players in the world. When a twelve-year-old French kid was improperly wiping the slippery floor, Patrick Ewing grabbed the mop and wiped the floor himself. The team took a break. Patrick Ewing was sitting by himself. Knowing how much Jack liked Ewing, I said, "Go over and say hello." Jack looked down and shook his head. *What?* My corporate husband was too shy to shake Ewing's hand? Maybe it was the same as me being too intimidated to introduce myself to Lyle Lovett.

"You go," he said.

"But I have nothing to say!" I said. "I don't even watch basketball." That didn't matter. I got up and walked over to Ewing, who looked at me. "Hi." I extended my hand. "I'm a huge fan." He grinned, then shook my hand firmly. His palm was bigger than a baseball mitt. "Good luck in the Olympics," I said, and returned to my seat.

Dinner that night was with the ten other invited guests, but to get to the ballroom, we had to walk through the hotel casino. I've always hated the sound of jingling and clinking slot machines and blackjack tables where stupefied patrons lose their money, but Jack loved to gamble. Fortunately, the few times we went to a casino, he'd place one or two huge bets and either win a pile of money or lose it all. Then we'd leave.

Suddenly, Jack stopped abruptly. His eyes turned into dinner plates as he looked past a velvet cordoned rope. "That's Michael Jordan," he whispered. "Can you imagine gambling next to him?" I peered at the table but couldn't see anything because a huge crowd of people stood in front of us. I'd never seen Jack that excited. He finally chose a blackjack table, won one thousand dollars on his first bet, cashed in his chips, and we went back to our room.

The next night, we were guests at the dinner Prince Rainier was hosting for the Dream Team. Our host knew I spoke French, so he sat me next to Prince Rainier. I couldn't believe I'd be speaking with the ruler of Monaco, but my joy turned to disappointment as they separated all the couples. Jack was seated with Christian Laettner, David Robinson, Larry Bird, and some of the other invited guests.

My table included Charles Barkley, Patrick Ewing, Karl Malone, Coach Chuck Daly, Chris Mullin, and Magic Johnson. I had no idea (except for Ewing) which team any of them played for. The seats on both sides of me were empty, though I knew one was for Prince Rainier. I hoped I wouldn't be stuck with the other seat empty. Worse, what could I talk about with these superstars? I didn't watch basketball and hadn't played since high school, back when there were six players and guards couldn't cross the center line.

A tall, elegant man dressed in a custom suit and silk tie and whose face was as familiar as a dollar bill took the seat next to me. He extended his huge hand and said, "Hello, I'm Michael Jordan." I could feel my face turn hot as I shook his beefy palm.

"I know who you are," I said. "But you've got the wrong dinner partner."

He looked at me quizzically. "Why do you say that?"

"Because, I hate watching basketball and squeaky sneakers, I can't stand golf and thwacking club sounds, and I detest gambling with all that clink-clinking."

He grinned and said, "We're going to get along just fine."

Suddenly, a man in a tuxedo raced from table to table and said, "Stand up! Stand up. The prince is coming."

Magic Johnson called across to Michael Jordan, "Hey MJ!"

"Yeah, MJ?" Jordan answered back.

"You think we should make people stand up for us?"

"Yeah, MJ, I do."

I needn't have worried about talking to Price Rainier in any language, because he seemed bored by the entire event and during the night said only one sentence to Jordan. I wondered how Grace Kelly could give up her career for him. On the other hand, I had Michael to myself. We talked about relationships and how separate bathrooms were the glue that cemented a happy marriage. I told him my husband had seen him gambling, and would it be okay if Jack joined him at the blackjack table?

"Of course," Michael said.

After dinner, we strolled around outside and then went to the casino, where once again, Jordan, along with Scottie Pippen, was gambling at a table protected by a velvet rope. I took Jack's hand and pushed my way past the people to the front of the rope. "Sorry," said the security guard, "this is private."

"We've been invited," I said.

"Sorry, madame, you cannot go in."

Michael was about fifteen feet away. "Hey, Michael!" I called. He looked up. I pointed to Jack. Michael nodded, and the security guard unhooked the rope. It was as though Moses had raised his hand and parted the Red Sea, and Jack gambled happily sitting next to Michael. Jack didn't win, but it was the happiest money he'd ever parted with and the most exciting gambling experience of his life. As for me, I'd sat next to Michael Jordan at dinner.

Let's face it. Life is too good to be true when you're living a fairy tale, and in my gut, I somehow knew my life was about to change in a very different way.

18

The Big Ditch

The first ten years with Jack were the happiest of my life. My company was doing better than ever, both financially and creatively, and the charity events were fun, especially the Ralph Lauren Folk Art benefit, whose dress code was "vintage velvet and lace." I wore my grandmother's Victorian white blouse, petticoat, and bloomers, and to my surprise, the *NY Post* published my picture.

While Jack worked on a deal to acquire RJR Nabisco, the managing partner of his law firm secretly contacted a different client to offer a competing bid. The managing partner was fired for creating a "Chinese Wall," and Jack was voted in managing partner. He was now on the phone every night working on RJR. His unwanted pounds crept back on, but when I tried to get him to return to Canyon Ranch, he said he was too busy. Instead, he sent me for an activity-filled week of hiking, aerobics classes, and a daily massage.

Jack was always extremely generous. For his daughter's marriage (three hundred people at the Pierre), he bought me a twenty-five-thousand-dollar Victorian locket of gigantic sapphires and diamonds and a Bob Mackie dress. Still, something was beginning to change—like the very attractive euphorbia plant, Jack could also be toxic. Cut the euphorbia even slightly, and a milky white poison drips out, causing severe skin irritation. In our eleventh year, I still ran the river each morning, but Jack had stopped. We hadn't played tennis in months because he was always busy. The only thing that remained the same were the endless charity events and dinners with his clients.

A month after he became managing partner, he said, "Tell me when I begin to believe my own press." I noticed he'd become short-tempered, less loving, and rather cocky, but when I tried to tell him, he didn't want to hear it. So, the less he listened, the more coke I did.

By now, I'd told him I did coke, and he knew when I'd done too much because I'd click my words and have to drink endless bottles of water. To prevent me from getting too high, Jack took over my coke management. When he decided I'd had enough, he'd hide it in his bathrobe, but he had no idea I knew where it was. When he was on the phone or in the shower, I'd tiptoe into the closet, stick my hand into his bathrobe pocket, and do a few more lines. And then a few more lines. And then I'd be so stoned I'd have to take an Ambien to get to sleep.

Every Monday, I'd meet my dealer near my office on the corner of Madison Avenue and Forty-Fifth Street to buy an eight ball, 3.5 grams of coke for three hundred dollars. From time to time, when I was too stoned to even watch TV, I'd tell myself I was done with this and throw the little glass bottle into the incinerator or fling it into our pond in Greenwich. But the very next day, I'd call the dealer and buy more because I couldn't function without it.

All the things I'd once loved were now different. Seeing the personal shopper for designer clothes no longer gave me pleasure. The charity events were all duplicates of each other—the same people, same speeches, same silent auctions. I was beginning to detest the endless social events, but I still had to attend and look great no matter what, because that's the role of a corporate wife.

One weekend in Greenwich, hoping to get him to start working out again, I bought two hybrid twenty-one-speed bikes, even though Jack hadn't ridden since his three-speed bike in junior high. We left the driveway and started to climb our first hill. I called out to tell him which hand to use and whether he should shift the gear forward or away from him. He couldn't (or refused) to master it and was so frustrated he got off the bike and walked it back home.

"I'll never ride again," he said.

"But I just bought the bikes!" I said.

"Guest bike," he answered.

I didn't quit working out even though he had. Every weekend, I'd go cycling as he stayed home, glued to the TV and phone. I loved pedaling the hills and flying back down them with the wind on my face. I could never persuade him to give his bike another try. But that wasn't the only problem. Even though I was working out like crazy, I, too, was gaining a few pounds from all the client meals. Jack could tell exactly how much I weighed by looking at my butt, just as an arborist can deduct the age of a tree by counting the trunk rings. He knew exactly if I'd gained two pounds or five, and as he wanted me to be perfect, he'd send me back to Canyon Ranch to lose the extra pounds.

I'd return home more fit than ever, and my weekend bike rides became longer. When I put the bike back in the garage, I'd always suggest he come outside and we'd go into the Jacuzzi.

"It's noisy," he'd complain.

"What is?" I'd ask.

"The birds," he'd respond.

He tried a new tact to keep me home: I'd be pumping air in my tires, and he'd suggest I have some cocaine before I left. I'd snort one line, then another, and then a third, which completely took away my desire to do anything except sit opposite him in the matching leather Eames chair. I'd turn into a zombie, barely able to move. And it happened more and more often. Every time I planned a workout, he'd ply me with coke. My habit became worse. To take away my hangovers, I began doing a few lines in the morning before work. I'd meet my dealer, go to the gym, and take a couple of hits before spin class, completely out of control. On the outside, I looked normal because no one knew I was doing it except Jack.

I nailed my newest and most prestigious client, Vidal Sassoon, who hired me to do a marketing video. I was so thrilled that when they asked if hair, makeup, and a wardrobe mistress were included, I said yes because I didn't want to lose the client.

The day before the shoot, I realized that with all these inclusions, I wasn't going to break even, let alone make a profit. I'd lose money. I took some coke to steady my nerves, called them, and said I was very sorry, but the shoot was off. The client was livid, but I didn't care because I couldn't possibly give them everything they demanded. Why not quit before it got worse? Had I not been so foggy, I would have been able to tell them that every new request would cost extra, and I'm sure they would have paid. But cocaine was a demanding lover that won every time.

I was more and more unhappy. It wasn't just the Sassoon shoot. I wasn't getting the same high, so I snorted more, chasing euphoria that never came. Now the coke would only last a few days, but Jack didn't care because three hundred dollars was nothing to him. The more I used, the more my nose would bleed or my nostrils would close up, and I could barely breathe. And even though I felt miserable every time I did it, I *had* to have that white powder.

Each day, I swore I'd stop, but I couldn't. I decided to do half as much, a decision that lasted less than an hour. A few years earlier, my good friend had died of an overdose, but she'd shot speedballs. That would never be me, because I'd never use a needle. Nor would I be the guy I once dated who had died of a heroin overdose. But I couldn't stop alone. I needed help. I looked up Cocaine Anonymous. There was a meeting Wednesday night, but that was three days away. I told a friend in Alcoholics Anonymous about my coke addiction, and she suggested I go to an AA meeting. "But coke is my problem, not alcohol," I said.

"An addict is an addict," she said.

Without telling Jack, I went to a lunchtime AA meeting and told the group I wasn't an alcoholic, I was a coke addict. Like my friend, they said an addict is an addict. I'd just bought a new eight ball and asked the group if I should sell it back to the dealer. They thought that was hysterical and told me to just get rid of it and not drink alcohol. I threw the coke down the incinerator May 21, 1995, and while I can barely believe it, I have not touched coke since that day, thirty years ago.

That night, Jack and I went to dinner alone—no clients. He didn't know I'd given up coke and drinking. We always laughed about his best friend's wife, who didn't drink; we called her the leper. Everybody we knew drank. Jack ordered a bottle of Talbot, but I told him I wasn't going to be drinking tonight. "Why?" he asked. I explained I'd given up coke, had gone to an AA meeting, and had been advised not to drink. I ordered seltzer water with a splash of Angostura bitters.

"Do you have to make it so obvious?" he asked.

"What?" I asked.

"Do you have to call so much attention to your not drinking by ordering the bitters?"

I didn't answer.

"So, you're giving up *everything*?" he said. He looked miserable, and I understood why. He was losing his drinking buddy.

Things went downhill from there. He hated me being sober. I was working out with a vengeance, because in AA they had suggested I double my workouts. My bike rides and runs were both longer—*anything* not to be stuck in the house. Then, just when I thought it couldn't get worse, Jack was invited by the

Securities and Exchange chairman to go on an invitational adult Outward Bound trip. It would be a weeklong adventure paddling the Colorado River in the Grand Canyon. Jack hated sleeping in anything but a plushy bed and wouldn't think of sleeping in the outdoors. Noise. Bugs. Dirt.

When I'd done my first Outward Bound trip in Lodore Cayon, the guides had said running the Colorado was the greatest adventure of a lifetime with some of the most exciting rapids in North America: Lava Falls, Hermit, and ABC, or ALIVE BEFORE CRYSTAL. I never thought I'd have the chance to paddle the Canyon because it takes years to get a permit. But what if I went in Jack's place? Jack thought that was a brilliant idea, because it would get him off the hook. The SEC chairman wasn't happy about the substitution but had to agree because Jack had been responsible for getting him short-listed for the job of SEC chairman.

The "Big Ditch," as they call it, is not just about paddling gigantic rapids. It's a place where you glide past billion-year-old red cliff walls rising thousands of feet into the sky. Each morning, I'd wake up at first light when the cliffs were blanketed in pink and lavender. By noon, they'd turn plum and russet, and in the late afternoon, a vermillion curtain spread across the walls. When the sun dipped, the walls glowed burnished copper and, in the moonlight, they turned silver. At night, I was mesmerized by a universe of stars, so close I could almost touch them.

I loved paddling the rapids from my perch in left bow, listening as our guide called out commands: "Forward! Left turn! Right turn! Back paddle!"

We'd dig our oars into the roaring froth using our thighs as leverage and gripping for dear life. The rafts would tear into the huge pounding waves and just miss the "sleepers," or unseen rocks. Then, safely through each rapid, we'd high-five with our paddles. During long stretches of still water, we'd drift along silently, lost in our thoughts. The guide let us take turns being captain, but none of us understood the river, and if one of us paddled, we'd inevitably end up in an eddy, a swirling circle of water that would trap the raft. To get back out into the current, we'd have to paddle till our arms ached.

That's how I was beginning to think of my marriage—like an eddy. We'd been so united against the world our first ten years, our respective dismal childhoods holding us together like glue. But these last two years, the glue was no longer holding. We were paddling in different directions. Jack no longer shared things that happened at work. He'd become sarcastic, and I'd become bossy. When had the negativity started? Was it because I'd given up coke so he could no longer control me?

Suddenly, there was a roar in the distance like a huge truck thundering down a gravel road. You heard the rapids long before you saw them, and the closer we got, the louder they sounded. I barely heard the guide as she screamed, "FORWARD," and we shot through turbulent gray waves, pounded and thrashed by thousands of metric tons of water. "BACK PADDLE," she cried, and we chopped at the waves as we swirled backward through the racing water, our raft like a rubber duck, bobbing helplessly. A spray of icy water slapped me in the face, and just when I was sure we were going to capsize, we bumped over the last big wave into a series of riffles and were safe. It was exhilarating.

One morning, I awoke to an explosive sound like a gunshot. *Bang!* I looked around, frightened. On a ledge just six feet above me, two bighorn rams collided head-on, butting horns. I reached for my camera, but my movement startled them, and they darted away. I knew if I told Jack about it, he would sarcastically say, "Isn't that special."

Later that day, we tied up the boats to tamarisk trees and hiked to a magnificent waterfall. I sat next to our guide and told her how sorry I was that I was only here for a week and not doing the entire river. I said Jack would have hated this, and if he had come, he would have found a way to get himself helicoptered out. He wouldn't like being wet and dirty, hiking over slippery rocks, sleeping on the ground, no hot water, no clean clothes, and no air conditioning. She asked why I was married to a guy who was so lazy when I was so adventurous.

"I'm in love," I said, but I wondered. Jack no longer touched me the way he used to, and it no longer felt like the two of us against the world. He'd become nasty since I'd stopped drinking and doing coke. Was he angry he could no longer control me?

The next day, we hiked up a steep trail to the Nankoweap Granaries, a row of square windows cut into the sandstone around AD 1100. Hunters and gatherers raised crops and lived here for thousands of years before the Canyon was discovered. It was shady, a perfect respite from the relentless sun. I felt happier and more peaceful than I had in a long time. I knew if I told Jack about this, he'd just pretend to yawn and say, "Ho hum."

That night I couldn't sleep. I was so mesmerized by the shooting stars and the moon rising above the cliffs that I was afraid if I closed my eyes, I might miss it. I was free here. I didn't have to live my life around his schedule. I could have put up with all the client dinners as long as he was his old loving self when we came home, but since becoming the boss, he was less patient and had become very edgy, not the man I'd married. I no longer knew who he was, and I realized I no longer loved him. The only solution was to leave him. But the idea of being alone, giving up my comfortable lifestyle, having to find my own apartment and start all over again at the age of fifty-two, was much too terrifying to imagine. Here in the solitude and beauty of the Grand Canyon, what had seemed so important before—the social status, the country home, the clothes, the car, his success—no longer made me happy.

My joy was paddling the rapids, watching the sun cut a golden swath through the water, sleeping under the stars, and daring myself to do things that had always terrified me, like the hike to Vasey's Paradise. Terrified, I had slid down a steep waterfall into the frigid water and then couldn't stop laughing. Even more thrilling was the day we all jumped off the raft into the river and swam through some rapids. After that, there was nothing that scared me.

Suddenly, it was our last night. The next morning, we'd hike up the Bright Angel Trail, and a new Outward Bound invitational group would hike in and do the second half of the river. How could seven days have gone by so quickly? We'd just done our last big rapid, Sockdolager, a roller coaster of nine huge waves that made me hunger for more big water. We tied up the boats at Lower Cremation, a strange name for a beautiful campsite with a 360-degree view of the massive red cliffs. Was this really the last night I'd sleep outside? Was Sockdolager the last rapid I'd do? The guide walked by and I told her how I felt.

"Why don't you stay?" she said. "The best rapids are in the Lower Half. Lava Falls and Granite and Crystal, the famous rapids."

"I can't."

"Look, you're already dirty, and you're halfway through, so you might as well stay on and finish the river."

I didn't have any projects next week, so I really could stay. But there were at least two dinners with Jack's clients, one Broadway benefit, and a cocktail party, and . . . oh my God, I'd almost forgotten Jack's birthday was next week.

"I've got to go home," I said.

"Okay," she said. "But if you ever come back, don't just do the first half. Start over again. That's the only way to get the full experience of the Canyon."

It had been an exhausting day. I carried my dunnage bag to the top of the hill and picked out a campsite. A couple of the guides planned to ferry across the river to Phantom Ranch, where there was a working phone. They asked if any of us wanted to go. I thought about going to tell Jack I wanted to stay for the second half, but he would never understand. He'd be angry, and not just because I wouldn't be home for his birthday. I'd better go home.

That night, I couldn't sleep. I didn't want to miss the best rapids of all. I should have crossed the river and called him, but he would have persuaded me to come home. Yet, if I didn't stay, I'd regret it for the rest of my life. I looked up at the thousands of stars. This would be the last night I'd see them. I would never get back here, and once home, all the tension would return. I pulled out my headlamp and wrote down Jack's cell phone number, then scribbled a note explaining why I was staying. One of my raftmates could call him after they hiked up to El Tovar Lodge tomorrow.

The next morning, I watched everyone start the long hike up. My heart was pounding, because I knew my life had come to the end of one rapid and was at the beginning of a new one—with Jack or without him.

19

The Separation

After leaving the river, we stopped in Flagstaff, and I looked for a birthday gift but couldn't find anything. I'd always made Jack's birthday super special—one year I threw him a surprise birthday party, another, I took him to Morocco. The best present was the year I made a video of his life, which began by superimposing his face on every popular magazine, including *Forbes*, *Time*, and *Newsweek*. He loved it. The next year, I made a video with his father talking about Jack. I included every home movie and photo of the young Jack, a filmography Jack could someday share with his kids and grandkids. But what to get him now? He didn't read books, just newspapers, he didn't need clothes, and there wasn't anything here in Flagstaff that he'd appreciate. I finally chose a little statue of an Anasazi ancient warrior carrying a spear. It wasn't very special, but with us not getting along so well these days, I didn't really care.

It was not a happy homecoming. Usually, when I returned home from a shoot or Canyon Ranch, I'd race into his arms and we'd close the bedroom curtains and tune out the world. This time, I'd been away fourteen days.

"Happy birthday," I said, handing him the little warrior.

He took one look at it and flung it across the room. Obviously, for him, staying on the river had been unacceptable. Our maid told me Jack had been miserable, and *how* could I miss his birthday? She said she'd desperately tried to get in touch with me but didn't know how, and I should have come home a week ago.

"Listen," I told her, "if a marriage can't last because I stay an extra seven days, then I'm sorry." Meanwhile, Jack was sulking in the den watching TV. "Why don't we take a walk?" I suggested.

"I don't want to take a walk," he said. He wouldn't even look at me. I had a feeling this relationship wasn't going to work unless I went back to being his drinking buddy.

That night, we went to our favorite restaurant in Greenwich, where we'd gone almost every Friday night for the last twelve years. We always ordered a bottle of Malbec, steak au poivre and pommes frites, and shared what we'd done that day. Not tonight. He didn't want to hear anything about the river. For a moment, I wondered if I should do cocaine, because he'd be much nicer if he could control me again. But I would never do coke again, because it turned me into someone I was not. Besides, giving it up had been as hard as giving up cigarettes.

We drove home in silence and went to bed. He wouldn't say a word, and when I tried to spoon my body against his, he brushed me away. I couldn't sleep, so I opened the sliding door to the back patio. Near the pool was a small rubber boat pool toy. I turned it upside down and used it as an air mattress. The night was balmy, and the wind caressed the pine trees. It felt good to be back out in nature.

I don't know how we got through the next day. He stayed in

the den watching sports. I went for a long bike ride, stopping at a little park with swings because flying through the air has always made me feel free. I am not a religious person, but I prayed to my Higher Power, whomever that might be, to please piece my marriage back together.

We ate dinner in silence and then watched a movie. After, he turned off the TV and went to bed. I planned to go back outside to sleep on top of the raft, but it started to rain. I could have gone into one of the empty bedrooms, but it didn't feel right, so I returned to our bed. I don't remember exactly what he said, but it was something particularly nasty and it came out of nowhere. That was it. How much abuse was I expected to take?

Without pausing, I spit out, "I want a divorce." I didn't really mean it, because I knew I'd never have the courage to actually leave.

When we returned to Manhattan, he said he wanted us to separate for a while. I didn't believe him. But he finally held me that night, so I knew he had to be bluffing. A week later, on Labor Day, he moved into a furnished sublet two blocks down the street. Maybe the separation would reignite the spark. We agreed not to tell anyone we'd separated. If anyone called, I was to say he was either in the office or the shower. Then I'd call him at his new place and tell him to call so-and-so. Texting hadn't yet been invented, so we were speaking a number of times a day. He continued to go to his charity events and dinners, but alone, making excuses for my absence. His clients must have thought I was dying, or I'd turned into a hypochondriac.

Jack wanted nothing to do with the Greenwich house, so I went there every weekend, mainly for the pool and my bike rides. But at night, I'd scream in misery at the top of my lungs. How could such a great marriage have turned so rotten? I changed the answering message from "Hi, neither of us can take your call right now" to "*No one* can take your call right now."

But gossip is the currency of New York, and even though we'd agreed to keep it private and joke about how long we could keep saying he was in the office, people looked at me strangely. I hadn't told my friends (not that I had many—mostly our friends were couples/clients). At work, my producer sensed something was wrong. She said I seemed different, even sad. One of my friends asked me if I had cancer, because I'd lost seven pounds in just two months.

I continued to go to the country on weekends. On the way back, I'd stop at the park with the swings. As I kicked and swung higher, I vowed we'd be back together after the last autumn leaf fell. But when the last leaf was on the ground, nothing changed. I was as lonely and unhappy as before.

Three months went by. I was still passing along his phone calls. He said one of his clients had seen him at a restaurant without me and had asked where I was. He told him we were living apart. That night, the wife of that client called me. She was one of those Botoxed-up-the-wazoo women to whom I'd never had anything to say. Her first words to me were, "I am *shocked!*"

"I can't talk to you right now," I lied. "I'm on the other line."

"Call me right back as soon as you're off." I didn't call back, so she kept calling, asking why.

"Look," I finally said, "I have no intention of discussing this with you." I hung up.

The only people who understand a separation are those who've been through one. And even they have no idea what to say. If you have a life-threatening disease, you get sympathy, but when you say you're separated, everyone inevitably says the wrong thing such as, "Oh, whose idea was it?" and "Who got the apartment?" or "Is he looking after you financially?" and "Are you selling the country house?" They aren't malicious, they just don't understand. One of my few friends took me out to cheer me up.

"It's not that you don't love him, it's just that you don't like him, right?" she offered.

"No, it's not that at all," I told her. "Just because *you* don't like your husband, don't project that on me."

Then there was the acquaintance who called and said, "Oh, I never liked him. You were smart to dump him."

To which I replied, "Do you think I want to hear the person I spent twelve years of my life with be criticized?"

The cruelest remark came from the mother-in-law of my stepdaughter, who said, "I certainly hope Jack has a prenup." The bitch.

The hardest question was, "Will you be getting back together?"

"I don't even know what I'm doing tomorrow," I'd say. "How would I know what's going to happen in the future?"

Every question was painful and inappropriate. I wish someone would have said, "I'm sorry and I'm here for you." But no one did.

Three months passed. Although I convinced myself the separation was temporary, I knew our marriage was broken. I hired a divorce lawyer.

"What do you want?" she asked.

"I want him back." I didn't really mean it, because we were now like two strangers.

"You don't need a lawyer," she said, "you need a shrink."

I lived my life as though any day he'd move back in—not the new Jack who'd become mean and abusive, but the old Jack whom I loved. I knew I'd never meet someone new, so maybe it would be better to patch things up. He'd taken just a few clothes. All over the bedroom wall were smiling photos of the two of us holding hands in Paris, Venice, St. Barth's, Cap d'Antibes, and Positano. Happier days.

The lawyer suggested a postnuptial agreement, which meant we'd put into writing what I would get in the event we divorced. Jack hired his own attorney. The weather turned colder. Our housekeeper moved his winter clothes to his sublet. His closet in our apartment was now empty except for a pair of leather dress boots I'd made him buy that he'd always hated.

Two more months went by. I missed him, and I couldn't understand why he'd changed for the worse. I took down the photos of us. The holes in the wall were the only thing left of our twelve years. I joined the Appalachian Hiking Club and drove the Porsche up to Bear Mountain and Breakneck Ridge and Harriman State Park. When he called to see how I was doing, I told him I was now hiking.

"You're crazy," he said.

I began to read at night, something I never did with him because the TV was always on, and I'd been too stoned. I joined the advisory board of Outward Bound and was invited on a hiking trip to Bhutan. I called Jack to tell him.

"Where's Bhutan?" he asked.

I said it was between China and India in the Himalayas.

"You're crazy," he said. "What are you doing that for?"

"Because I want to," I said.

Finally, I didn't have to make up excuses or not do something because he didn't approve.

We went ahead with the divorce. He said I was entitled to half of everything he owned, that I'd earned it. But the money was unimportant. I was lonely. This was long before online dating. I didn't meet anyone when I went to dance clubs. A friend suggested I try a dating coach named Julie, so I called her. Before we could meet, she said I had to write down three things I wanted in a man and three things I've always wanted to try. For the man, I wrote intelligence, a sense of humor, and openness. For things to try, I listed rollerblading, scuba diving, tap-dancing, jewelry-making, and adventurous vacations.

Julie arrived at my apartment. "Now, the first thing is, you have to be open," she said. "Every man you meet is a potential new partner. You have to look at men even as you walk down the street. Smile. Don't be afraid." *Easy for her to say*, I thought. Beneath my supposed confidence, I was terrified. "I am going to give you a MAP," she said.

"Of the city?" I asked.

"No, Mate Action Plan. Do not rule any man out. You never know when the short, bald guy you didn't like will fix you up with his brilliant, funny friend. Now let's see your interests." I handed her my list. "You certainly have a lot. I'm going to give you three things to do and you're to call me when you've done all three. The first thing I want you to do is go to a jazz concert."

"It's not on my list," I protested. "And I only like Dixieland."

"Men like jazz," she said. "And besides, there's a benefit coming up with a cocktail party. It's only thirty-five dollars, and it's tax deductible."

The night of the jazz concert, it poured. I arrived dripping wet and spent the entire first act trying to thaw out. During intermission, I cruised the lobby, but no one approached. After the concert, I went to the cocktail party. I knew no one. Bored, I perused the dessert buffet. The room eventually filled up. I looked around and spotted a good-looking man at the dessert table, so I walked over, took a piece of pie, and got up the courage to say, "Great desserts, aren't they?" He smiled. Just when I was thinking how easy this was, he turned and sat down next to a pretty woman. I felt ridiculous. During the next hour, no one spoke to me, so I ate a brownie, a strawberry tart, and tried the chocolate mousse. The server looked at me. "What an extraordinary appetite you have," he said.

My second assignment was to go to Randall's Island on the shuttle bus and hit golf balls. "But I don't play golf," I protested.

"Trust me," Julie said, "men love golf."

I was not happy as I boarded the shuttle. Three women already seated glared at me. Julie must have sent them as well. There was a golf club on the seat nearest the door, so I moved the club and sat down. A handsome guy boarded the bus. I smiled at him. He said, "That's my seat. I left my club there." I moved and sat glumly in the back.

At the driving range, there were plenty of men, but none gave me so much as a glance. I bought a bucket of balls, rented a club, and hit balls uneventfully. Golf was simply not my thing. I left, the only passenger on the return bus.

The third activity was a political fundraising breakfast. "Men like politics," Julie said. "And please buy a piece of 'conversation jewelry' to wear at the breakfast. Get a real knockout piece. Men use offbeat jewelry as a conversation starter. I promise you, it will work."

The breakfast was a sit-anywhere, so I chose an all-male table except for two empty seats. I fingered my glittering necklace and said to the man next to me, "Hello, what brings you here?"

"I'm a freelance consultant," he said.

Unemployed, I thought. Worse, he shoveled food into his mouth the entire time he was talking. A woman sat in the empty seat next to me and said, "What an unusual piece of jewelry!" Turns out Julie got one thing right—just the wrong sex.

I called Julie. "So far, I've spent thirty-five dollars on the jazz concert, twenty-five on golf, and a hundred and thirty-five on the political fundraiser. Not only is this not working, but I've gained weight." There was silence on the line.

"I'm really disappointed," she finally said. "You have such a negative attitude. Naturally, you didn't meet anyone because you didn't have an open mind. Now, let me give you three new things to try. Call up the New York Triathlon Club."

"But I don't swim fast," I said.

"Then volunteer. Think about it. They'll finish all sweaty and dirty, and you'll look absolutely fresh and luscious."

I was no longer listening, but she'd given me a great idea. Why *not* try out things I'd always wanted to—not to meet a guy, but to get myself out of my funk. First, I tried underwater running with a swim coach who had flyers announcing an upcoming triathlon in Cuba. While thinking about that, I entered a twenty-five-mile bike race. I injured my hamstring and couldn't run, so I joined a race-walking club in Central Park.

I signed up for a "Writing from Personal Experience" workshop. My piece was about climbing a ropes course at a spa in Upstate New York, where I'd gone a few weeks after the separation. The students and teacher loved my story and suggested I get it published. But how? I had no idea where to start.

I continued with my new activities: I took the Porsche to Skip Barbers' Defensive Driving School in Lime Rock, Connecticut, and learned how to downshift on hills instead of using my brakes. I took a roller-blading lesson in Central Park, but didn't like it because I was so afraid of falling. I bought a ten-dollar pair of tap shoes and tried a beginner's tap lesson at Steps, but I couldn't follow, and the instructor was so frustrated with me she stopped giving me encouragement. I joined the YMCA and got scuba certified. I drove to the Shawangunk Mountains in New Paltz and hired an instructor to go rock climbing. I booked a four-day tennis camp led by Stan Smith at Hilton Head Island and actually won one point off of him. I met no one in these new activities, but that didn't matter. I was learning new skills, and some of them would help me later in my career, including getting scuba certified.

One day, I decided to volunteer for the Fifth Avenue Mile, running with the five- to seven-year-old Achilles runners. I stood near the start line, waiting as the media group was lined up to go next. Wait! Who was that blond curly-headed guy? It was a lawyer with whom I'd often played tennis.

"Miles?" I called out.

He turned. "Margie? What are *you* doing here?"

"I'm volunteering. What are you doing with the media group? You're a lawyer."

"Not anymore," he said. "I bought *MetroSports*. I'm a publisher now." *MetroSports* was a free magazine I'd seen at my gym and in athletic shops.

"Can I write for you?" I asked.

"Sure, send me something." The starting horn sounded, and Miles took off in a sprint.

A week later, I sent Miles my article on climbing a ropes course at a spa in Neversink, New York. He phoned to say he loved it and planned to publish it. Did I have any other pieces to send him? The magazine didn't pay, but it was a perfect way to build up my clips (published articles). Now, instead of trying to drum up new video clients, I sat at my desk and churned out stories. Miles promoted me to adventure sports and travel editor, gave me a business card, and assigned me to a Class of the Month column.

I wrote about a surfing class on a huge balance ball, I sweated my way through Powerstrike, did power yoga, and planned my Outward Bound adult invitational trekking trip to Bhutan. Life no longer felt so bleak. And the following week, when I went to REI to buy my camping gear for the trip, my life was about to change once more in a wonderful new way.

20

Sunflower: Brian

As I entered REI in New Rochelle, the assistant manager bounded toward me with a smile so big and warm he reminded me of a sunflower.

"May I help you?" he asked.

He was tall, muscular, and gorgeous, and I could feel myself blush. I could tell he was feeling something, too. I showed him my packing list, and he led me to the sleeping bags, explaining the difference between down and synthetic. He suggested I buy one good for minus-twenty degrees. I barely heard him. I was smitten. He spread a sleeping bag on the floor.

"Try that. Just zip yourself in." He smiled.

I was tempted to ask him to zip himself in with me, but said nothing. There was definitely a spark.

By the time we'd chosen hiking shoes, backpack, trekking

sticks, down parka, and raingear, I'd learned his name was Brian Smith, he was from Davenport, Iowa, was divorced, and had six brothers and sisters and a ten-year-old daughter named Sara, whom he missed. She lived in Davenport with her mother. I let it slip that I was separated and told myself not to be attracted to him, because it was obvious he would move back to Davenport at some point to be with his daughter.

I loved his hearty laugh. He was wearing khaki shorts and had the most well-toned calves I've ever seen. He had to be a runner and a hiker; he'd be a lot more fun to hike with than the Appalachian Mountain Club members. He picked out a fleece hat with a brim that covered the ears and closed with Velcro at the neck.

"This is really ugly," I said.

"You're going to need something that warm," he insisted. "I promise you." I took the hat, and he carried all the other items to the checkout counter. As he rung me up, he said, "Do you want to go kayaking with me tomorrow?"

"I'll go kayaking with you if you'll go hiking with me," I said.

"Deal." He grinned.

Sunflowers are a symbol of happiness, loyalty, and strength. That was Brian. He was fifteen years younger than me, and when I told him I was fifty-three, it didn't bother him in the least. A week after our hike/kayak day, he invited me on a tour of Lyndhurst, one of the finest historical mansions in the Hudson Valley. After the tour, we sneaked around to the back and climbed the fence to Washington Irving's home, Sunnyside. The sun was setting over the Hudson, cutting a golden swath through the river.

He looked at me and said, "May I kiss you?"

"I thought you'd never ask," I said.

It was a loving and long kiss, the best I'd ever had. We climbed back over the fence and sat on a bench overlooking the river. He kissed me again. We lay down on the bench together, making out like teenagers. His touch made me shiver. I hadn't felt this happy in a long time, and I only wished he could come on my trip with me.

I had plenty of time to think about him in Bhutan. Fifteen of us trekked along winding dirt paths surrounded by fragrant rhododendrons, crossed bridges over gurgling streams, and walked through fields where Bhutanese men cheered, booed, and hooted at each other as they played archery. We huffed and puffed up and down snow-covered mountains and visited monasteries in the middle of nowhere where monks as young as five sat rigidly, chanting for hours.

One day, we climbed up to the Tiger's Nest Monastery perched three thousand feet off the ground and ten thousand feet above sea level. It was freezing and snowing, but the ugly hat Brian had persuaded me to buy kept me toasty and dry.

Another day, we were headed toward Bhutan's most sacred mountain, Jolmohari. The faster hikers were ahead and the slower ones way behind. I was alone and somewhere in the middle when a group of uniformed elementary school children appeared out of nowhere and ran toward me. "Hello, hello!" They waved their arms excitedly, showing off the one English word they knew.

"Kuzuzangpo la," I replied, my only Bhutanese word, for hello.

They crowded in, touching my clothes and grinning. And then they burst into a Bhutanese song, a tune I recognized from Girl Scout camp. When they finished, I sang the same tune in English with the hand movements: *"Do your ears hang low, do they wobble to and fro, can you tie them in a knot, can you tie them in a bow?"* I tied an imaginary bow in the air. *"Can you throw them over your shoulder like a Continental soldier?"* I pantomimed throwing something over my shoulder, saluted, then pulled on my ears again. *"Do your ears hang low?"*

They screamed and clapped and pulled on me, begging me to sing it again. We sang the song together—me in English, them in Bhutanese. I taught them the hand movements. They wanted a second song, so I sang "Rocka My Soul in the Bosom of Abraham." I wanted to stay and sing every song I knew, but soon the sun would set. I waved goodbye and continued up the trail, grinning and feeling lighter than I had all day. That's what travel meant to me—special moments like this.

When I returned to NYC, Brian greeted me with a bouquet of flowers and said, "Beautiful flowers for a beautiful lady." Jack had always sent me a dozen yellow roses on my birthday, Valentine's Day, and whenever I won an award, but it wasn't the same because Jack's secretary always ordered the bouquet. Brian brought me flowers in person.

Jack wanted nothing to do with the Greenwich house, so Brian and I stayed there every weekend and used it as a base for our many adventures. Every time I wanted to do something daring, Brian was up for it. After, we'd return to the house, light a fire, and cuddle on the living room rug.

A few months after the Bhutan trip, an Outward Bound instructor called to say there'd been a cancellation for an invitational Mt. Rainier climb, and there was a space if I wanted it. I increased the distance of my morning run and did hill repeats in Central Park. Brian came over lugging a huge backpack and weighed it down with four five-pound bags of flour. He made me climb up and down the steps of my thirty-three-floor apartment building at least twice daily. When I wanted to give up, he'd climb the stairs with me and make me laugh. Every week, he'd increase the weight until I was climbing with thirty-five pounds, the amount I'd have to haul up the 14,410-foot-high mountain.

A week before the climb, I met with the editor of *Spafinder* about a marketing film. I told him that besides being a filmmaker, I was a writer and would love to do a spa story for him. He wanted to know what I had in mind, and I told him I'd probably go to a spa to recover from climbing Mt. Rainier.

"You're climbing Mt. Rainier?" he asked.

"In a week," I said,

"*That's* the story I want," he said.

It was my first feature for a major magazine. When I arrived at Rainier and met the other climbing guides, I found out that one of them, Carl Skoog from Bellingham, Washington, was an adventure photographer who climbed with a Nikon large camera strapped to his chest. Now I'd have great photos for my story. While climbing, I tried to smile for the photos, but each step was a grueling experience. We were roped together, and I was last. At one point, my foot slipped into a crevasse. I screamed and tried to self-arrest with my ice axe. Fortunately, all my teammates dug their axes into the snow and were able to stop my fall. It never occurred to me that over 450 people die climbing this unforgiving mountain either by falling into a crevasse or slipping off the mountain.

By the time we finally summitted, we were all exhausted, yet we still had to descend. Most climbing accidents happen on the way down. My legs felt like Jell-O, my pack was like lead, and when the sun rose, the snow turned to slush. I slipped and fell, and my teammates had to dig in their axes to stop me from tumbling down the mountain. I fell a second time, and the instructor said, "I thought you practiced climbing stairs? What's going on?" I was too embarrassed to admit I'd never bothered to climb *down* the stairs. I'd take the elevator down and climb back up.

Due to a snowstorm, which made it impossible to start out at midnight, it took twenty-one hours from base camp to the summit and back. When we finally arrived in the parking lot, I kicked off the miserably uncomfortable plastic mountaineering boots and wet socks. My feet were covered in blisters, but it was over—and we'd made it, even though only 60 percent of guided hikes summit. Best, now I would have my first cover feature in a national publication.

Back home, Brian was so proud he had a trophy engraved with my name and summit date. In the 1990s, there was a section in *The New York Times* called "The City," and I submitted my essay about climbing the thirty-three flights of stairs while training for Rainier. It was published. To celebrate, Brian had a second trophy made for me.

Everything about Brian was genuine. I didn't miss the lifestyle with Jack—not the fancy dinners or designer clothes or fake friendships. Brian offered a life full of love, fun, and adventure.

He suggested we go camping on New Year's Eve, which sounded horrible and cold, but he promised I'd love it. We drove the Porsche to Harriman State Park and started up a snow-covered trail. I had at least thirty pounds in my pack and could barely stand, let alone trudge through the snow. After an hour, Brian began to swear because, according to his map, we should have already reached the shelter. He charged ahead to find it, and I found a little clearing where I could sit for a moment.

When I tried to stand back up, the pack threw me off balance and I fell on my back, the heavy pack cushioning me. I was now a bug, hands and feet in the air. I tried but couldn't turn over sideways.

"BRIAN!" I screamed.

No answer. He was too far ahead.

I crawled backward and tried to sit against a large rock. Inch by inch, I pushed until finally I was standing. Whew! Eventually, I arrived at the shelter, where Brian had already set up our tent and was cooking dinner on two camp stoves: a delicious spicy stew on one and homemade banana cake on the other. With our sleeping bags zipped together, we celebrated the silent New Year in each other's arms, far away from the madness of Times Square.

A few months after that, a client sent me to El Salvador in the Bahamas to do a public service announcement about saving the oceans starring Jean-Michel Cousteau, son of Jacques. Good thing I'd learned how to scuba, or I never would have been able to take on the assignment. I was not yet certified, and it was my first real dive other than the YMCA pool. The underwater sea life was mesmerizing—an otherworldly experience with undulating purple and yellow coral, fish of every variety and color, and sea turtles who seemed to swim in slow motion. After the shoot, I flew to Sarasota to get scuba certified. The ocean was rough, and the other participant upchucked into his regulator. I managed not to throw up and somehow was able to climb up the boat's ladder even as the waves swelled. I passed the test even though I was positive I'd fail, and it made me realize there was nothing I couldn't do, no matter how scary.

Brian invited me to come to Davenport for Christmas and meet his family: there was his father Smitty, Smitty's partner Howard, his three sisters Suzi, Beege, and Shannon, his three younger brothers, Kevin, Chris, and Kerry, and his daughter Sara. There was also a gaggle of adorable grandchildren. As the plane flew over Davenport, I expected to see endless fields of corn, but there were none. Davenport was a thriving town along the banks of the Mississippi. Brian's brothers and sisters, each as sweet and loving as Brian, greeted me with smiles and warmth. Smitty was dressed up as Santa Claus and, one by one, the grandkids sat on his lap. A few months before, I'd told Brian I'd never sat on Santa's lap because my parents didn't have the money. But now, Brian lifted me up onto Santa's lap and we laughed until I was crying. The Smiths made me realize what I had always longed for—a loving family.

Brian and I spent a second year of weekends together in New York. My video production company was thriving, and my writing career was taking off. *Walking Magazine* assigned me to do a marathon in Honolulu, all expenses paid. Brian, who had been running with me for weeks, insisted on coming to keep me company.

At 5 a.m., as Brian and I walked to Honolulu's start line, I began to cry. How could I possibly go 26.4 miles? Brian hugged me and promised he'd meet me every few miles. And he did. He'd show up, kiss me, and tell me to keep going. He was there at mile 22 when many hit the wall, but with his encouragement, I made it to the finish line and got my medal. Without my knowing, he had done the entire marathon, always staying just behind me.

That spring, Brian and I kayaked to David's Island, the previous site of Fort Slocum off the coast of New Rochelle. When we pulled our kayaks out of the water, Brian sat me down and explained he couldn't let Sara grow up without him. He needed to move home and would love me to join him. Would I move with him to Davenport? My company was here, and I didn't want to leave it or Manhattan. Saying goodbye to Brian was gut wrenching, but he promised he'd come visit, and I could come there anytime. And I would, because I not only loved him, but his entire family as well.

Weekends without Brian were desperately lonely. I returned to hiking with the Appalachian Mountain Club, but it wasn't half as much fun. I missed Brian. By now, Jack and I had agreed to sell the country house, so pretty soon I wouldn't have a weekend home. I replaced biking the backcountry Greenwich hills with those of Central Park. I injured myself running, so I joined a racewalking club.

It was 1996. Jack and I signed our divorce agreement. He would pay the rent on the NYC apartment for a year, then I could either take over the lease or move out. Pay five thousand a month for a three-bedroom apartment I didn't need? No way! I looked for a smaller, cheaper place in Midtown, but everything either needed to be gutted or was too expensive. I wanted Midtown East because it was halfway between the river and Central Park, my two outdoor gyms.

One Saturday morning, my alarm failed to go off. It was too late to join the racewalkers in Central Park, so I headed for the East River. Racewalking is a very weird-looking sport. Unlike walking, you waddle like a duck because one heel must touch the ground before you can lift the other foot. It looks ridiculous, but it's much more injury-free than running.

I was charging along the East River pathway when suddenly I heard a *swoosh swoosh swoosh* behind me. I turned. A guy with a red nylon jacket was pumping his arms, racewalking. WHAT? Nobody racewalked except me and my little group. Being the competitive person I am, I surged ahead, leaving him in my wake. Feeling smug, I kept going. Suddenly, there he was again—*swoosh swoosh swoosh*. I smoked him once more, but he wasn't giving up. Now we were side by side and I had no wind left. Not to lose face, I sputtered out, "You're very good for my pace."

"And you're very good for mine," he said, equally winded.

There were only two possibilities: one of us was going to pull ahead, or we could stay together. So, just making conversation, I said, "What do you do?"

"Real estate," he said, slowing down his pace, thank God.

"Commercial or residential?" Me, still making conversation.

"Residential. I work for Douglas Elliman. Are you looking?" I told him I'd given up. Everything was either too expensive or needed too much work. "What are you looking for?" he asked.

"Two bedrooms, a wood-burning fireplace, huge sunny windows, and a terrace, in this neighborhood."

"Do you want to look with me?" he said.

"No," I said, "because I know it's hopeless. But, if you ever find my dream apartment at an affordable price and your clients don't want it, let me know." I gave him my address.

The next day, the doorman sent up a note on Douglas Elliman stationery. He said he'd found my perfect place—just four blocks from where I presently lived. There were two bedrooms, a huge living room, wood-burning fireplace, dining alcove, two bathrooms, a windowed kitchen, and a built-in laundry room. There was no terrace, but who cared? It sounded perfect, but I didn't get excited because I knew when I called back, he'd tell me it had just sold. And if I went to see the place, it would probably face a brick wall or be next to a construction site. But you never know, so I called and asked to see it. The owner didn't want anyone on a Sunday, he said, but I could come Monday morning. I knew that by then, he'd say it was sold.

I had no expectations when I walked into the Fifty-Second Street brownstone and went up the elevator to the fifth floor. He unlocked the door, and my heart dropped. Spacious, yes, but the wooden floors were painted dark brown, the walls were dark blue. Track lights dangled precariously from the ceiling. The windows were huge, but they were so filthy you couldn't see anything. Somewhere behind those windows was the view of a courtyard with trees as high as the apartment. The place had no terrace, though it had everything else I wanted, including its own laundry room. But it was disgusting.

"All it needs is a good coat of white paint," he insisted.

I didn't trust my judgment, so I brought in the Greenwich decorator. "Grab it," she said, "It's a gem."

My Outward Bound mentor, who owned a Tudor City triplex, came to look. "You'd be insane not to buy it," he said.

Even my accountant said it was a steal. It had never been in my plans to buy an apartment, but I wasn't about to move to Davenport, and certainly buying a place of my own would be an excellent investment.

Signing the lease terrified me, but I did it anyway, trying not to have a panic attack. I gutted the space and decorated it with my souvenirs from around the world. Now, twenty-five years later, every morning, I sit in the living room and read the newspaper as the sun pours in through the gigantic windows. In the winter, I make roaring fires. My co-op is presently worth at least four times what I paid, but I will never move out because this will always be my sanctuary.

So here I was with my brand-new apartment, but once I'd moved in, organized my files, and hung all the art, I no longer had busy work; on the weekends I was lonelier than ever. What difference did it make having the perfect apartment and best job in the world if I didn't have Brian to share it with? I needed something to fill the hole, and I knew I could mope and wait for something to happen or go do something about it. So, I did.

21

Poppy: Hope

Most divorced women have children to keep them company. Not me. I never wanted kids. When people asked, I'd say, "Oh dear, I forgot to have children," which I'd once seen on a T-shirt. And it wasn't that I didn't like other people's kids, it was just that I didn't know any. Then I learned about Big Brothers/Big Sisters of NYC, a mentorship program that matches up children ("Littles") with volunteers ("Bigs"). The idea of spending some time with a young girl seemed like a good way to assuage some of my loneliness, as you met them only a few hours each month. It wasn't like adopting a child full time, it was being a mentor. It would give me a chance to show an underprivileged kid a different world.

They matched me with Hope, an eleven-year-old seventh grader at PS 131 in Chinatown who lived with her grandmother in the Harlem projects. Hope's mother lived in Staten Island and was on drugs. Her father, now with a new wife and baby, constantly made plans to visit Hope but never showed up. As both Hope and I needed somebody, I anticipated a preteen who would love the attention I'd shower on her. She bounded into the school library, a thin olive-skinned girl with dark eyes as big as saucers and a long, dark ponytail. She smiled, revealing a mouth full of silver braces. She reminded me of a poppy, a highly prized flower that can be either extremely easy or maddeningly difficult to grow.

"Hope is a beautiful name," I said. "How'd you get that?"

"Well, Mommy was going to have three kids and name them Faith, Hope, and Charity, but she named my older sister Venus instead. Venus is my half-sister and her and her son Joshua live with us. He's autistic but he's so cute. You'd love him!" Her face lit up. She and her ten-year-old sister Mimi slept head to foot in the same bed and Mimi was always kicking her. The grandmother shared a bed with Hope's aunt's child in the same room.

"How long have you been living with your grandmother?" I asked.

"Since I was five."

"What's it like?

"She's sick all the time with asthma and a lot of times she has to go to the emergency room." She looked at me and said, "No little girl should have this much pain. I have such a black hole in my heart."

I wanted to hug her. "Listen, Hope," I said, "if you can survive this, you can survive anything."

She replied, "That's what my sister Venus says." She paused. "Are you married? Do you have a family?"

"I'm divorced, twice," I said. "I have one sister. Both my parents and older sister are dead."

Oh, you have it hard," she said.

"So do you," I said. The school bell rang. "See you in two weeks?" She stood up and gave me a little hug. It was the first time I'd smiled since Brian left.

Two weeks later, Hope and I sat in the school library trying to make conversation. "Do you like school?" I asked.

"I hate it," she said.

"Not even gym?"

"I hate gym," she said.

"So, what do you do for fun?" I asked.

She shrugged. "Watch TV."

"What else?" I asked.

"Nothing. I get bored."

"Do you play with your grandmother?" I was trying to make a joke.

"My grandma's fifty-seven years old," she said. "She's too old. What do *you* do for fun?"

I didn't mention I was a year older than her grandmother. "I have a video production company," I said. "I travel a lot, and I write too. I work out. I'm on the boards of a modern dance company and Advertising Women of New York. And I'm an advisor to Outward Bound."

"Wow," she said. "You must do twenty things." She looked down. "I have to ask you something I'm kind of ashamed of."

"Yes?" Was she going to tell me she didn't want me as her Big Sister? Was I about to be rejected by an eleven-year-old?

"Um," she said. "What's your name? I forgot it."

I was so relieved I laughed out loud.

With permission from her grandmother, I was able to take her out on Saturdays. Our first trip was to Central Park, where we rode the carousel and played on the swings. We sat and I read her the first chapter of *Charlotte's Web*, then handed her the book. Her reading was fourth-grade level, and she couldn't pronounce the farmer, Mr. Zuckerman. I told her to call him Mr. Z. That worked.

Another time I took her to the Bronx Zoo, where she had never been, and she lit up and screamed with excitement every time she saw an animal, especially the polar bears. I wanted to take her away for a weekend, because the best way to get to know someone is to travel with them. Hope had never been out of Manhattan or stayed in a hotel. I decided to take her to a chocolate factory in Massachusetts, but it would have to wait.

I'd been hired by *Elite Traveler* magazine to go to the British Virgin Islands for a story on Peter Jennings, Anne Randolph Hearst, and Governor Winthrop Rockefeller, members of the BVI Trust. The editor had been looking for a writer who was a certified scuba diver because Jennings would dive. My diving certification was paying off in spades.

After I returned home from the BVI, I picked up Hope for our first road trip. She slid into the Porsche passenger seat with her backpack. "Wow," she said. "This is such a beautiful car."

"Thank you," I said. "My ex-husband didn't want it."

"WHAT?" she said.

"He wanted a touring car, so he bought a Mercedes and gave this to me." I turned on the radio. "So, what kind of music do you like?

"I loooovvvee Alisha and JLo, but my favorite is Ja Rule."

"Who's Ja Rule?" I asked.

"YOU DON'T KNOW WHO JA RULE IS?"

"I know he's a rapper," I said. "And I think he swears every second word and calls women 'hos.'" (Little did I know that many years later, I would do a feature on Ja Rule for a business magazine. He was a gentleman and never used the "ho" word once.)

"You gotta listen to Ja Rule," Hope said. She flipped the dial to a hip-hop station and after a while, Ja Rule came on. "Here he is!" she screamed. She sang every word. I didn't like Ja Rule's putting down women, but he had some original things to say. Maybe Hope had a few things to teach me. It was a three-hour drive, and when we finally reached the city, Hope looked up at every building and said excitedly, "Is that it? Is that it?"

"Not yet," I said. She was so stoked about going to a hotel that she couldn't sit still. Finally, we parked and took our backpacks to a hotel room with two double beds.

"Oh my GOD!" Hope scampered on top of one of the beds and jumped up and down. "I have my own *bed*? I don't have to sleep with Mimi kicking me in the face?" She jumped off the bed. "OH MY GOD. A TV AND A REMOTE! OH MY GOD, A REMOTE!" Then she noticed the coffee maker. "WHAT?" she said. "Is that just for US?" I nodded.

She reached for her phone. "I gotta call Grandma!" She ran around the room, phoned her grandmother, then jumped up and down on the bed again.

For dinner, we went downstairs and sat at a table with a tablecloth and cloth napkins. Hope unfolded the white linen square and held it up. "Margie, what's this for?"

"It's a napkin," I said. "Some restaurants have cloth napkins."

"Why?"

"Just to be fancy."

"Can I take it home?" she asked.

"I don't think that would be a good idea," I said.

The next morning, we drove to the chocolate factory, where the entire staff in uniform were lined up, reminding me of the servants lining up at Downton Abbey. The manager groveled and said we could make whatever we wanted. We each chose the easiest—chocolate on a stick decorated with sprinkles.

When we left, Hope said, "Margie, why they be ass-kissing you like that?" I explained that because I was a writer, they wanted to be sure I wrote good things about them, so they always gave me the royal treatment. Then Hope said, "Margie, how old are you?" I knew the jig was up.

"I'm fifty-eight," I admitted, expecting that to be a dealbreaker.

"You ARE?" she said. "OH MY GOD. You do so much! I don't believe it." And then she said, "Aren't you Jewish?"

"Yes," I said.

"Well, where are your horns?"

"MY HORNS?" I said.

"Your horns. My grandma told me all Jews have horns."

"Of course, Jews don't have horns. That is ridiculous," I said. I knew exactly where I was taking her on our next road trip. "Listen, Hope, there's a lot of prejudice in this world. Jews don't have horns, and I'm going to prove it to you. Have you ever heard of Nazi Germany and the Holocaust?" She shook her head no. "Did you learn about a man named Hitler?"

"No. Who's he?"

"Hitler was an evil man who ruled Germany. He wasn't Jewish, and he hated Jews, so they became his victims. He sent six million Jews to death camps and killed them all. Hitler was the devil, not Jews. I'm going to take you to Washington, DC, to the Holocaust Memorial Museum. You'll see that Jews have never had horns except in ugly cartoons."

A month later, Hope and I took the train to Washington, DC. We would stay at my friend Shelby's house. The Holocaust Museum had many screens with films showing Jews being packed into trains, their skeletal bodies shivering in the concentration camp bunkrooms, dead Jews thrown into open graves, and other atrocities. I couldn't stop sobbing.

"Margie, I'm bored," Hope said.

"This is important," I snapped. "We'll go when I'm ready." Hope looked at me sullenly. I made her stay another half hour watching the horrifying images. "Okay," I finally said, "we can go now."

We were headed to the exit when I saw a group of kids enter a room with a sign reading, "Daniel's Story."

"What's that?" Hope asked.

We entered the room. The exhibition was about Daniel, an eight-year-old Jewish boy who lived in the ghetto and was forced to go on a packed train with his parents from whom he was separated the moment they arrived at the camp. Daniel was made to take off his clothes for a shower, but instead of water, he was gassed and killed.

Outside the exhibition was a counter with paper, crayons, and a sign: "WRITE DANIEL A NOTE." Hope wrote in big block letters with a red crayon, "Dear Daniel, I am so sorry for what happened to you." Beneath it, she drew a red heart. She looked at me and said, "It wasn't fair what happened to Daniel. He was just a little boy."

"It wasn't fair what happened to any of them," I said. "All six million."

"But they couldn't kill that many people," she said. "It's not possible."

"I'm afraid it is," I said.

"Wait till I tell my grandma," she said.

I wondered, would she tell her grandmother that six million Jews had been killed? That Jews had no horns?

Hope and I continued to meet every other week. She turned twelve. For her birthday, I planned to take her on a gentle hike near the Hudson River. We were to meet in front of her apartment. I waited in the car, terrified because I had the top down and this was not a safe area, especially for a blond in a Porsche. Ten minutes went by. I called the apartment. No answer. I waited, then called again. Still no answer. Finally, I locked the car, walked to the front entrance, and buzzed the apartment. Her sister Venus answered and said Hope had gone to her uncle's house for the weekend. I was livid. I explained that Hope and I had a date.

"Next time, have *me* come," Venus said.

I sulked for a week. Maybe I should have checked in with her the day before. I called her the following week and said I'd come by Saturday to pick her up. Again, she didn't show up. Disappointed, I called her that night. "I'm sorry," she said, "I forgot."

When I got off the phone, I began to cry. How could a twelve-year-old upset me this way? I called my friend Judy, who had two grown sons and four grandkids. When I told her, she said, "Kids will break your heart." A few weeks later, I suggested that Hope and I go to Central Park's Conservatory Garden. We'd meet at the 105th Street entrance. She stood me up.

The Big Brothers/Big Sisters program manager said if a Little fails to show up three times in a row, it's over. She said that Hope was now at an age where she was more interested in boys than a big sister, and I shouldn't take it personally. But I did. I'd lost Hope, and I lost hope—that is, until I suddenly had an idea that would once again change my life.

22

Changing My Life Again

Having been rejected by a twelve-year-old, it was time to do something productive. My video production company, which I'd now had for ten years, no longer gave me the joy or creative high I craved. As I'd finally earned enough money to support myself for a year, I dissolved MG Productions and became a full-time freelance writer.

There was a blurb in a newsletter about Travel Classics, a conference in which travel writers had one-on-one meetings with magazine editors. I called the founder, Maren Rudolph, but she said the conference was full. I begged. I pleaded. I told her I'd sleep in a closet or pitch a tent outside. I promised her a dozen fresh NYC bagels. But to no avail. She told me to apply the following year.

I don't give up. I called her every day for three weeks until finally someone cancelled, and I was in. I picked up twelve freshly baked bagels and headed to Troutbeck in Amenia, New York. Maren Rudolph was effusive about the bagels. It wasn't until years later when we became good friends that she admitted she hated bagels.

The Travel Classics conference jolted my writing career into fifth gear. I nailed assignments from *Distinction* (now defunct), *Modern Bride* (now defunct), *National Geographic Traveler* (now only digital), *Executive Traveler* (now defunct), *Global Business Traveler* (now defunct), and *Affluent Traveler* (now defunct).

The editor of *Elite Traveler* called and said she wanted me to write an ongoing feature called "Fourteen Days for the *Elite Traveler*." It could be fourteen days in Japan, or South Korea, or New Zealand, or Vietnam, and it included the most high-end hotels, private drivers and guides, gourmet meals, and business-class air. I began living life beyond my wildest dreams. And I'd done it myself.

Still, every time I came home from a trip, I was lonely. I longed for a lasting relationship, but how could I have one when I didn't hang out in bars and didn't know where to find someone? By now, everyone was using dating apps, but I was much too ashamed to expose myself online. What if someone I knew saw my photo?

I spent my free time working out. Every morning, I'd either do a run in Central Park or ride my bike, treating myself to the swings afterward as a reward. I was on the swings one morning when a group of eight women ran into the playground, led by a female instructor with an Australian accent. She shouted orders, telling them to run up and down the seesaws, do tricep and bicep dips off the benches, and drop for crunches. Everything they did looked hard but fun, so I clomped over in my biking shoes and asked the instructor who they were.

She handed me a flyer and said, "Join us." The group was called Shape Up with Simone and met twice weekly at 6 a.m. in the park. I joined, and the other members soon became my friends. We did half-marathons and adventure races together, had parties, and shared meals. Life was fun again and, for the next two years, we trained with Simone, who'd come every summer to escape the Australian winter. What we didn't know was that Simone was bipolar, and one winter in Melbourne, she ended her life.

Our little group trained together for a while but eventually broke up, so I joined a triathlon class called Terrier Tri. We biked and ran in the park and swam in the Equinox pool. Most of the members were in their thirties, forties, and fifties, and I was already sixty-five. But there was a wonderful camaraderie and no one cared I was the oldest and slowest.

My first Olympic-distance triathlon was in Cuba, followed by the New York Triathlon, then the New York Marathon, then a funky adventure race called the Urbanathlon, which I won for my age group. I told everybody, "Of course I won. Everyone else my age is dead."

Between my travel assignments and workouts, I was no longer miserable, but still had pangs of envy whenever I saw couples holding hands or kissing in restaurants. I ached for intimacy but had no chance of finding it unless I tried online dating. First, I had to create a profile. Ugh, what would I say about myself? I tried to keep it simple, knocked ten years off my age, looked for the most flattering photos I could find, stalled for a week, and finally pushed "Send."

Ping. My first bite, Roger, worked in the DA's office. We spoke on the phone, and he didn't sound like a serial killer, so we met for coffee. He wasn't bad looking, but he kept talking about himself. Thirty minutes elapsed. He was still blabbing nonstop. I pretended I was sick and left. Next was Walter, who'd posted a picture of himself twenty years younger and thirty pounds lighter. Then there was Jay, who could only communicate by telling jokes and was offended I never told any. This was definitely not going to work.

Just when I was about to delete my account, a man named Marshall emailed, a scientist who lived in Bellport, Long Island,

and worked as a climatologist at Brookhaven Lab. I loved his Texas accent. He sounded smart and up for adventure. I couldn't take any more Starbucks coffee dates, so I suggested we hike Breakneck Ridge near Cold Spring, New York. At least if I didn't like him, I'd have someone to hike with. Marshall kept up on the trail and couldn't have been more easygoing, but there was no chemistry.

Amazing how quickly that changed. Maybe because it was summer and he lived close to the beach, or maybe because he was a train ride away, which meant we'd only see each other on weekends because I wasn't ready for anything more than that. But in spite of my not being attracted, we ended up in bed together—and shockingly, he was amazing.

Marshall wanted to learn Spanish and suggested we take five weeks off and join an immersive beginner's Spanish course in Oaxaca. I'd never taken off five weeks, but was always sorry I hadn't learned Spanish, so why not? We flew to Mexico, stayed in a cheap apartment, bought fresh food from the local market, and listened as vendors in little wheeled carts walked the streets shouting, "Tamales, tamales, tamales!" Every day we went to classes at an Oaxacan language school. After four weeks, we rented a VW bug and drove six hours to Zipolite, a sleepy beach town.

Our cheap bungalow was ten steps from the sea, and at night we could hear the waves roll in. Marshall and I never said, "I love you," because neither of us did. But that didn't matter, because I finally had someone to be with. He didn't mind that I sometimes traveled for weeks because he, too, went on long expeditions to test his climate instruments.

Marshall was the perfect person to take to the Marquesas Islands. He knew how to keep himself busy on the cargo/passenger boat and, when we docked, joined me on the steep hikes. It wasn't a perfect relationship, and it could be rocky at times because we were both stubborn. Often, we'd crawl into bed furious with each other, but there was still fantastic sex.

In the middle of our second year together, Marshall was on a ship somewhere in the Horn of Africa, due back in Seattle late December. I planned to throw myself a party on my birthday, January 3. I'd never thrown a big party before, but I knew Marshall would be there to help, so I invited forty people. Just after Christmas, Marshall emailed. He was off the ship, visiting his family in Seattle, and would fly to New York in a few days.

He didn't give me his arrival date, so I called to find out. He said he was too tired and wasn't coming to NYC. I was livid. I threw his clothes into a cardboard box, emailed him, and told him to have his clothes picked up and FedEx my keys back immediately.

"You don't really mean that," he emailed back.

"Oh, yes, I do," I wrote. "And if your clothes aren't gone in two days, I'm throwing them out."

It wasn't as painful as breaking up with John or Jack, and I wasn't heartbroken as I had been when Brian moved away, but it was still hurtful.

Marshall might be gone, but I was still getting assignments to exotic places with posh hotels, and even though there were always two fluffy bathrobes and iced champagne for two, I was no longer upset about being alone. To challenge myself, I combined every luxe trip with something adventurous and frightening. Eleanor Roosevelt said, "Do one thing every day that scares you." And I did. Once, I deppelled (upside-down rappelling) over a gorge in New Brunswick. Another time, I circumnavigated the top of the 1,749-foot-high Toronto CN Tower. One of the scariest was cycling the trail on the rock-strewn island of Grand Manan in New Brunswick. It was so steep, I often had to pick up my bike and carry it up the hill. Going back down, I fell and developed an egg-sized bump on my shin, but couldn't have been prouder.

I was never lonely on international trips. Being transported to a new culture always made me forget about everything else. No matter what country, children called out, "Hello, hello," the one English word they knew. I learned to say it back in Chinese (*NEE-how*), Korean (*Anya-SAY-o*), Vietnamese (*Sin-chow*), and about ten other languages. But that was the only word I knew, so I could never have a real conversation.

Then I had an idea. There is a universal language that requires no words, and that is music. If I could learn to play an instrument small enough to carry in my pocket, I'd be able to interact with the locals. Then I remembered thirty years earlier I'd taken a harmonica lesson in San Diego from the author of a blues harmonica how-to book. I googled his name and up popped Jon Gindick's Blues Harmonica Jam Camp.

I called him. He remembered me and begged me to come to jam camp in Clarksdale in the Mississippi Delta, where raw beginners were welcome. Participants would stay at the Shack Up Inn, a funky hodgepodge of reconstructed sharecroppers' shacks. I flew to Memphis, rented a car, and drove towards Clarksdale. Were those real cotton fields? I pulled to the side of the road, walked to the edge of the field, and picked a fluffy white ball off the stem. Even if I hated jam camp, I'd never seen real cotton before. This moment alone was worth the trip.

The other jam campers came from all over the country, as well as Australia and England. We laughed our way through every class and meal. Learning was also fun, and by day three, I knew what a twelve-bar shuffle was. I learned about blues harmonica greats I'd never heard of before—Little Walter, Sonny Boy I and II, and Big Walter Horton. I'd known nothing about the blues.

Each morning I'd get up, run through the cotton fields, have breakfast, and go to class. After dinner, we'd listen to live blues in Clarksdale, including one of the last authentic juke joints, Red's, where famous blues harp player (that's what people call the harmonica) Charlie Musselwhite was sitting right next to me on a barstool. I was much too intimidated to talk to him, though a few years later, I would interview him twice. For graduation, we were each to play in front of a live audience at Morgan Freeman's Ground Zero Blues Club. I can't think of anything more frightening than playing in front of people, except maybe a tax audit. It was my turn, I got up on stage, and when I blew my first three notes, my knees finally stopped shaking. I only played for about thirty seconds, but after, a few people approached me and said they couldn't believe I'd just started. Their encouragement nourished my spirit, and when I returned home, I started weekly Skype lessons with Lee Edwards, a wonderful blues harp teacher in Wales. (If you're wondering what a Welshman knows about the blues, the answer is, plenty).

A few weeks after jam camp, I was assigned, "Fourteen Days in Turkey" for the *Elite Traveler*. After Istanbul, I went to Cappadocia, where I sat in a park watching children chase each other around the swings. They stopped, stared at me, and let me take a picture.

"*Merhaba*," I said. They smiled.

I took out my harp and played a boogie-woogie. They inched closer. When I finished, they applauded and indicated they wanted more. I played "Down by the Riverside," and they jumped up and down, then followed me out of the park as though I were the Pied Piper. I couldn't stop smiling.

Since then, I have played harmonica everywhere, including in Namibia for a Himba tribe, Papua New Guinea for the chief, and in a small village in Borneo. I joined a female drum corps in Caraquet, New Brunswick, for the yearly Acadian celebration, blowing my fool heart out for two straight hours. Twelve years ago, a friend told me about Big Ed Sullivan's World-Famous Jam blues jam Monday nights at the Red Lion on Bleecker Street, the oldest continuing blues jam (going strong for thirty-one years) in New York City. You bring your instrument, sign up, and they match you up with other players.

Armed with my harmonica case (a Bazooka lunch box I bought on eBay),) I signed up at the Red Lion, sitting close to the stage, where the house band was performing. After a couple of songs, Big Ed Sullivan (who co-runs the jam with Grammy-nominated singer/songwriter Christine Santelli) looked at me and said, "Are you a singer?"

"No, I'm a harp player," I said.

They continued to play. A sax player named Chuckie got up with the house band and killed it. Was I crazy? I couldn't possibly play like these guys. The room filled up quickly, and a new band was called to the stage. I sneaked over to the whiteboard, erased my name, and walked out the door. Big Ed Sullivan was standing there. Busted.

"Leaving so soon?" he said.

"I'll come back when I can play like you guys," I said.

"Just play like you," he said.

I kept taking lessons online. Playing this little instrument brought me joy, even though I didn't practice enough to sound half good. I learned about an organization called SPAH—not the fluff and puff kind but rather, Society for the Preservation and Advancement of the Harmonica. Here, master harmonica players such as Kim Wilson, Rick Estrin, Jason Ricci, Magic Dick, Joe Filisko, and so many other greats gave workshops (and signed my harmonica case). I began to write pro bono for SPAH's magazine, *Harmonica Happenings*. The interviews didn't make me a better player, but I was in awe of how many thousands of hours each of these pros had practiced.

The following year, I returned to harmonica jam camp, but this time, two of my friends, Patty and Debbie, wanted to join me. While neither of them loved taking up harp, they loved shopping, so I'd go to class while they shopped the entire day. With my new passion for the harp and all my trips, meeting a guy was no longer important. And then, the most unbelievable thing happened, something that would never have been possible if I hadn't taken my friends and didn't play harmonica.

23

Gardenia: JR

A few months after harmonica camp, I learned that Dennis Gruenling, a harmonica rock star, would be performing at a NYC blues club. I don't like going to music events alone, so I dragged Patty and Debbie to join me. Patty wore her Shack-Up Inn T-shirt, which I thought was pretty gutsy because, as a single woman, you couldn't *pay* me to wear that. At the entrance, a tall, distinguished man took our tickets.

"Welcome," he said, as he noticed Patty's T-shirt and asked, "You've been to the Shack-Up?" He had a thick Southern accent. I love a man with a Southern accent, even though it ended up the *only* thing good about Marshall.

"Yes," she said. "We went to harmonica jam camp in Clarksdale."

He looked at Patty, amazed. "You play *harmonica*?" he asked.

"No," Patty said as she pointed to me and said, "but *she* does."

He looked at me. "You play *harmonica*?"

"Yup," I said. "Blues harp."

"Wow!" he said.

After the show, he was again at the entrance and, as we were leaving, asked me why I'd taken up harp. I explained. He told me he'd produced this show, and he loved the blues. He was handsome and smiled easily. His name was JR. *Interesting*, I thought. *Another J, just like John and Jack.* He asked if I wanted to be on his mailing list for future blues shows, and I gave him my email. Patty and Debbie sensed I was staying, so they left. JR told me he lived in a suburb of New Jersey. I figured he had to be married, because not many single people live in the suburbs.

The next day, he emailed to say that a blues festival, "Maplewoodstock," was taking place in New Jersey on Saturday, and asked if I wanted to go. Maplewood was only a thirty-minute train ride from Penn Station. If he was inviting me, that must mean he was single.

He was waiting at the train station. We walked across the street to the festival, where a number of bands played, and then the blues star Shemekia Copeland took the stage. JR told me she was Texas singer/guitarist Johnny Copeland's daughter, but I'd never heard of either her father or her. (Not many years later, I would meet and interview Shemekia twice.) At this point, I knew nothing about the blues except what I'd learned at jam camp. JR, originally from Georgia, had moved to Montclair, New Jersey, was divorced twice (just like me), his daughter from his first marriage lived in Charlotte, and his daughter and son by his second marriage both lived nearby with their families.

After the concert, he waited with me at the station. He was so gentle and sweet, and I could feel the chemistry. When the train arrived and we said goodbye, I expected him to kiss me, but he didn't. He called the next day, saying he had tickets to a blues concert in the city. Did I want to go? Yes! He asked where I'd like to have dinner, and I suggested Bond 45, my go-to theatre district restaurant, and close to the venue. During the meal, he told me why he loved the blues.

He reminded me of a gardenia "Fortuniana" a strong, handsome, rounded gardenia with attractive white, scented flowers that symbolizes love, purity, and trust. When the check came, he paid in cash. I found that strange, because the only people I ever knew who did that were drug dealers, and he obviously wasn't. As we walked over to the club, he told me all about the various blues artists he'd seen. He was an encyclopedia of blues information, and his voice was seductive. I was smitten.

After the show, we walked to my apartment and he told me he'd worked in reinsurance (I knew from Jack this was a very lucrative field), but a year earlier, his two partners, who owed him eight million dollars, refused to pay him. He'd already spent five hundred thousand on lawyers. Didn't he have a contract, I asked. He said, "In the South, we do it on a handshake." That was the strangest thing I'd ever heard, but what do I know about how they do business in the South? He said his two partners had now moved to London, and he couldn't afford to start a new lawsuit. This would explain why he'd paid for the restaurant in cash; he obviously had no credit cards. "I have no money," he said.

"That doesn't bother me, because I have my own money," I said. Later, when he dropped me off at my building, he still didn't try to kiss me. I was surprised, because it wasn't as though we were teenagers. I was sixty-nine and he was seventy-two.

The following week, he invited me back to New Jersey to watch the summer Olympics on TV. He was waiting at the station in a brand-new BMW, and we drove until he pulled into the driveway of a huge house whose interior was sumptuously decorated. I told him I loved his home, and he said, "It's my daughter's home. She and her husband are out of town, so I come by daily to walk the dog. Thought it would make sense to eat here as well."

He made a delicious ceviche, followed by spareribs he'd marinated all day and slow-cooked on the grill, the best spareribs I've ever tasted. After, we sat on the couch and watched women's gymnastics. I tried to move my bare arm so it touched his, but either he didn't feel it or didn't take the hint. As it was almost 11 p.m., he insisted on driving me home. During the trip, he told me the car belonged to his daughter. The fact that we'd been in his daughter's home and were now in her car didn't bother me, because it had been a long time since I'd been this attracted to someone. He pulled into a parking space in front of my building.

"Want to come up for a cup of coffee?" I asked.

"Sure," he said. As soon as we stepped into my apartment, he kissed me, a long, perfect kiss. And then, just like that, he picked me up in his arms and carried me into the bedroom. No one had ever done that before. He was a generous and passionate lover. Afterward, we lay there, and he held me in his arms.

"So why didn't you even try to kiss me before?" I asked.

"Because I'm a Southern gentleman," he said.

We spent the following weekend at his home in New Jersey, a small, drab house whose floors creaked. His bedroom was upstairs, so small you could barely fit two end tables and a queen-sized bed, but I didn't care because I really liked him. The next morning, he made a delicious breakfast. His son and daughter-in-law dropped by with their five-year-old, obviously to check me out. I could tell they approved. When they left, they both said, "I love you," to JR. Then we drove to his daughter's and son-in-law's house, which I'd already seen. I liked them both and could tell by the way they exchanged smiles with JR that they approved of me. When we left, they, too, said, "I love you," to JR, and he said it back. There was so much warmth in that family. Except for Brian's family, whom I adored and had stayed in touch with, this was all new to me. My father had never said, "I love you," and my mother only said it the day she called me in Paris.

JR and I spent all day Sunday locked in each other's arms. As he drove me to the train station that afternoon in his very old SUV, he told me he had a motorcycle and asked me to join him on a ride to Bear Mountain the following weekend. All I could think of were tattoos, black leather, chains, and falling. But he was persuasive. He said we'd go up the West Side Highway toward the Cloisters, and if I didn't like it, we'd turn around and go right back home.

The following weekend he arrived with an extra helmet and a woman's protective jacket. His bike was not a Harley but a sleek BMW R1200GS. He snapped my helmet closed, hopped on the bike, started the engine, and told me to get on. As we weaved our way through traffic, I clung to the sides of the bike for dear life. But he was a careful driver, and after a few blocks, I was no longer afraid. It was fun taking up so little space that we could pass every car. On the far west side, he pulled into a BMW dealership. Why? I wondered. As if reading my mind, he said, "You need a pair of protective gloves."

He thumbed through a display of women's leather gloves.

"Why do I need gloves?" I asked.

"To protect your hands," he said. "I'm wearing gloves, and you need them too."

The cheapest gloves were $150. This was a guy who had no money, yet he paid. I thought it was a complete waste of money for what I was sure would be a very short ride. But back on the road, instead of gripping the sides of the bike, I wrapped my arms tightly around his torso, which was not only sensual but made me feel safe. As we drove up 9W, I looked at the Hudson River and the scenery on the other side of the road as well. A car doesn't give you unobstructed views, and you never have the chance to see anything if you're driving.

We were heading up the winding road to Bear Mountain, and he told me to lean in the same direction he did. This was thrilling. I couldn't believe how freeing it was to be out in the open air, taking in the views. I was hooked. We had lunch at the Bear Mountain Inn, and I asked what he did with his time. He said he worked for his daughter's company, looking over the accounts. She paid him enough money for rent, gas, and food.

Hmmm, I thought. This made him free to travel with me, and it wouldn't cost me anything because my hotels and meals were always comped. Even better, with JR accompanying me, I would no longer have to eat alone.

The first trip I invited him on was for a story on Asheville,

North Carolina. I flew and JR went by motorcycle because he had plans for us after Asheville. It's a long drive by motorcycle, but JR's an "iron butt," which means a long-distance rider. They gave us a car to get around in Asheville, and I was thrilled he both drove and navigated. Had I been alone, I would have gotten constantly lost and would undoubtedly be screaming at the top of my lungs, because that's what I do when I'm lost. But with JR all I had to do was enjoy the scenery. I was a queen!

Later, we returned the car and left Asheville by motorcycle to drive the Tail of the Dragon, known as the curve capital of the world, eleven miles and 318 curves of Smoky Mountain asphalt (that's twenty-nine curves per mile). When we arrived at the entrance, JR pointed out the "Tree of Shame" festooned with various motorcycle crash parts. I was ready to bail, but once we got going and were leaning into curve after curve, I was ecstatic and couldn't get enough.

That was the beginning of many trips together, all of which I wrote about. My favorite was by motorcycle to the Romantic Road of Bavaria, a stunning country lane in Baden-Württemberg where there wasn't ever another vehicle in sight and where every ten miles or so we'd pass a church with a gorgeous onion-domed tower. Uncannily, the road was originally built for Hitler's tanks, but a clever German marketer changed its name to the Romantic Road.

We planned another motorcycle trip from San Francisco to Yosemite. JR's daughter said she'd pay his airfare, but I felt funny about that, so I paid instead. We were getting everything else free, plus I had so many airline miles that it rarely cost anything. Life with JR was magical, not only visiting his kids and their adorable children, but especially the trips we took together for my various assignments. There was a Burgundy river cruise on a posh barge that slept only six couples. We were the happiest couple on the barge, even kissing on our hot air balloon ride. There was the gorgeous river cruise up Portugal's Douro River, where we watched the world go by from our balcony and held hands whenever we deboarded. It was so nice to have someone with whom to share the fluffy hotel bathrobes and slippers. Back home, I'd stay in my apartment and write during the week, and on the weekends, commute to his house, often spending time with his family.

His daughter had just given birth to a second baby boy, and when we went to the hospital, she gave me the newborn to hold. I'd never held a brand-new baby before or been with a family who constantly said "I love you" to each other. Now they were saying it to me, too, and I said it back. Everything was different about this relationship. I'd never told John or Jack how resentful I'd become by being the obedient little wife. JR and I made a pact—we would always tell the other what was bothering us, no matter how trivial or ridiculous.

One day in the fall of 2014, I went to Rye, New York, with my friends Patty and Debbie for lunch. My stomach had felt gassy all morning, and I was mainlining Tums. We ordered lunch, but I suddenly doubled over in pain. Patti drove me to the train station, and fortunately, a train pulled in almost immediately. But I was in horrible discomfort, and at Grand Central, I grabbed a taxi and went to the emergency room of Weill Cornell Hospital. They took an x-ray, said I had a blocked bile duct, put in a stent, and sent me home.

The next morning, my stomach was killing me more than before they'd put in the stent. Back to the ER to learn the stent had become infected. They replaced it with a new one and did an MRI. That's when they discovered I had a small cancerous pancreatic cyst and would need a Whipple. I thought that was something nuns wore on their heads—no, that's a wimple. A Whipple, also known as a pancreaticoduodenectomy, is a complex four-to-six-hour operation to remove the head of the pancreas, part of the small intestine, the gallbladder, and the bile duct. This procedure kills 25 percent of those who have it. JR was in New Jersey, and I thought I was going to have to go to the hospital alone. I started to cry, just thinking about how alone I was, but my sister, Lynne, and her partner, Howard, sent me a little note, insisting on taking me. That made me cry even harder because Lynne and I were never very close.

Fortunately, my brilliant pancreatic cancer surgeon at Memorial Sloan Kettering Cancer Care saved my life. But after the operation, I felt as though a horse had kicked me in the gut. It was difficult to turn to my side, and I was in constant pain. JR came to the hospital and sat with me. On day three, I could walk a full lap around the hallway, and the fourth day, we took the elevator to the arts and crafts room and brought back a little wooden truck kit and paints. JR glued the truck together, painted it with a curly-haired blond driver in the driver's seat, and wrote on the side, "Margie's Moving On." It was the most creative gift I've ever received.

Every day, Lynne and Howard came to visit, and JR stayed with me and slept in my apartment. The only time I wasn't in pain was when I pushed the morphine drip button. By now, I could walk eight laps around the corridor, even though tubes were attached from my body to my IV pole, and every step hurt. I knew if I didn't keep moving, I'd atrophy. After eight days, they took out the tubes and released me. JR went home to New Jersey to catch up on work. The night I came home, I woke up at 2 a.m. to the most horrible diarrhea I'd ever experienced. I called the ER, and they said come in immediately. Turns out, the hospital had gifted me with both ESBL, a nasty bacteria, and C. difficile, a germ that causes severe diarrhea and colitis. That was the bad news. The good news was that because I was so contagious, I'd get a private room at no extra cost.

A few days later, I was released. I hired a day nurse and every day we'd walk; at first a few blocks, then more, and by the fifth day, I was up to seven blocks. I walked on the bus stop side of the street because there were benches, and every few blocks, I needed to sit down and rest. For twenty-five years, I'd been walking and biking Second Avenue, but until now I didn't realize it was so hilly. A week after I was home, I went to see the pancreatic surgeon, who was stunned by how quickly I was recovering. I'm not a superhero, but the best thing you can do after any operation is keep walking, and that's what made me heal so quickly.

But the surgeon gave me some terrible news—even though my nodes were negative, he wanted me to make an appointment with an MSKCC pancreatic oncologist, who recommended I do six cycles of chemotherapy to decrease the chance of the cancer returning.

"Why?" I argued. "My nodes are all negative."

"Because it will give you a 15 percent better chance of it not recurring."

I didn't think 15 percent was much, but Lynne and Howard begged me to do chemo. As they are my entire family, I gave in. The chemo was as bad as the Whipple. I felt listless and sick, and constantly had nausea. On my week off from chemo, I returned to the Travel Classics Writer's Conference, this time held in Scottsdale, Arizona. The night before the conference, I checked into the hotel but was thirstier than I've ever been in my life and began to shiver. Even a steaming hot bath didn't warm me up. I ended up in the emergency room of the hospital in nearby Cave Creek, completely dehydrated and with a low white blood cell count. They gave me an IV and released me after a few hours. I didn't tell anyone except a good friend I'd met my first year at the conference. She wanted to see my scar, so I lifted up my shirt, revealing a red line with little staple holes on each side. The unhealed scar started underneath my navel, hooked around it, and went all the way to my breastbone.

"Ewwww," she said. "It looks like you've been in a knife fight."

Hey, people, please think about what you say to victims of an operation. We're very sensitive and certainly don't want to hear things that are hurtful.

The scar finally healed. I survived the Whipple, was working out again, and my life was back to normal. Little did I know my life was about to radically change again—both in a truly wonderful and absolutely horrible way.

24

Bali and Beyond

Six weeks after the dreaded Whipple surgery, I could sit at my desk and write, work out with my triathlon team, and play some blues harmonica again. I dared myself to go back to Big Ed Sullivan's World-Famous Blues Jam, but this time I didn't cross my name off the list or sneak out. I played two songs with one of the bands, with a solo on each. It was terrifying to play in front of an audience, but I did it anyway, and when I got off stage, Big Ed was standing there smiling.

"Did you have fun?" he asked.

I said yes, relieved I hadn't made any major mistakes, but I didn't really have fun; it was frightening because all the other musicians were so good. It would be a very long time before I learned "Compare, despair, and stopped making it a competition.

At least I felt competent with my writing. *Business Jet Traveler*, a prestigious magazine for private jet owners, assigned me stories. The editor, Jeff Berger, was the toughest editor I'd ever worked with. He'd catch at least four mistakes in each submission and told me to proofread everything three times. I did, but not once did I manage to turn in a typo-free assignment. Happily, Jeff always forgave me. One of my assignments was to test-drive a brand-new Continental GT V8 Bentley convertible. JR and I decided to take it to the Finger Lakes. I was so scared of denting the $251,000-plus supercar that it took me thirty-five minutes to merge into Lincoln Tunnel traffic.

JR kept saying, "Go now!" But I was terrified some truck would smash into us. As the Finger Lakes was a good five-hour drive, I had plenty of time to think about what to call JR in my stories. "Boyfriend" made me sound like a teenager, "beau" sounded silly, and I didn't like "companion" or "partner." I decided to call him "my man." He was growing on me in a very positive way—easy to be with, loved to cook, and he was teaching me plenty about the blues. I didn't care that he had no money, because I'd learned the hard way that having a man with money didn't guarantee love.

When we arrived at Cayuga Lake, JR began to hint about marriage. He attended church every Sunday and explained that marriage is one of the basic tenets of family and church. All I could think was that during my first two marriages, I'd compromised on what I wanted. I didn't plan to ever do that again. Why get married?

For Thanksgiving, JR and I visited his daughter in Charlotte. She led us to the bedrooms of their fourteen- and sixteen-year-old daughters and put us separately in their bedrooms. JR explained that the family was very religious, and unless we were married, we couldn't sleep in the same bed.

A month later, I was assigned a travel story in Bali and planned to bring JR. When I told him, he began to laugh.

"What's so funny?" I asked.

"I have an idea," he said. "Why don't we get married in Bali?"

Hmmm, I thought. Surely, a marriage in Bali wouldn't be legal, so why not? And if we were married, his daughter in Charlotte would finally let us sleep in the same bed. When JR was in the shower, I called Jack, with whom I was now on friendly terms. I said, "If I married JR in Bali, it wouldn't count, right?"

"Listen," Jack said, "I don't care if you're married by a witch doctor. It counts." And then he added, "Marry him. Why not?"

Why not, I thought. I'd never had a *real* wedding. The first marriage was in a Mexican judge's dusty office, and the second at a fancy restaurant under an exit sign. This would be a traditional wedding at his church, and I'd get to walk down the aisle. We discussed the details. JR wanted to cut down his father's wedding band to make me a ring, but I loved my great-grandmother's thick gold wedding band engraved, "H.L. to S.L. July 6, 1884." A few years ago in India, I'd bought a gorgeous tanzanite and decided to have it set it in my great-grandmother's ring.

A driver picked us up at the Denpasar Airport in Bali, and we drove past stalls selling everything from sarongs and fans to tiles and baskets. We passed lush green rice paddies sandwiched between temples and more stalls before arriving at the COMO Shambhala Estate. Our suite's bed was draped with a gauzy canopy, and the terrace overlooked endless rice paddies. For a week, we toured Bali, had side-by-side massages, lazed at our private pool, and even took part in a spiritual ceremony. The following week, we flew fifty minutes to the pristine island of Sumba, undoubtedly what Bali must have looked like fifty years ago when there were no tourists. Here, there were only horses and goats polka-dotting the countryside.

We arrived at NIHI Sumba, the island's only luxury resort surrounded by a one-mile crescent-shaped beach. Our huge villa had a front lawn with a swing hanging from a tree branch, a shady outdoor dining area, and a private pool. In back was a second dining area overlooking the Indian Ocean and an outdoor king-sized bed in case we wanted to sleep under the stars. Our private butler attended to our every need, including waiting on the beach with two fluffy towels when we came out of the water. One day, she drove us to visit an ancient village, where all the children posed for the camera before racing to the SUV and giggling hysterically because they weren't used to seeing their reflections.

One night, we were dining by candlelight when JR dropped down on one knee and read from a scrap of paper: "*Saya Akan Mencintaimu Selamanya, Tolong Jadilah Bagian Dari Kehidupanku.*" He translated the Balinese words: "I will love you forever. Please be a part of my life." It was the most exotic and beautiful proposal of my life. When we returned to our villa, our bed had been decorated with the initials M and J in flower petals.

It was so romantic I was tempted to get married right there, but we would wait so JR's family, my sister, and her partner, Howard (who would walk me down the aisle), could attend. While in Bali, I decided to submit our story to *The New York Times* Wedding Vows section. The online request form said, "Tell us about your love story and how the proposal happened." I spent as much time filling it out as I would writing a feature story

When we returned to the States, Jack, being the shrewd lawyer he was, insisted I have a prenup, which JR was perfectly willing to sign. This meant JR and I saw each other's net worth. I couldn't believe how little he had to his name. His lawyer asked him if he wanted any money if our marriage ended. No, JR said. He was marrying for love. So was I. The wedding was now just a few weeks away. I bought a cream-colored lacy Calvin Klein dress and sparkly shoes with kitten heels (I have NEVER been able to wear high heels). And then, just when I'd forgotten about it, *The New York Times'* Vows editor called. There were endless questions from the *Times* reporter. A few weeks later, both the reporter and a photographer attended our perfect wedding (even though JR's Southern daughter later complained that our kiss at the altar was much too sensual). *The New York Times* team also attended our reception at JR's daughter's home, a feast of Brunswick stew and spareribs that JR had FedExed in from Georgia. A week after our wedding, the story appeared in *The*

New York Times with a huge headline, "Roaring Down an Unlikely Path to Romance."

For the next six months, life with JR was ideal. For one assignment, we spent Mardi Gras in New Orleans on Harry Connick's float (I would later interview him for a story) and went to a music festival in Quebec, where I heard my favorite, Lyle Lovett and His Big Band. For an assignment to the Republic of Georgia and Russia, they didn't offer to let me bring my new husband, so I went alone and brought with me thirty harmonicas, courtesy of Hohner Music. My guide arranged a visit to a fourth-grade class in the Caucasus, where I gave each student a harmonica and a short harmonica lesson. They were so excited they wouldn't take the instrument out of their mouths, and as I was leaving, they each made me sign their harmonica's cardboard case, as if I were a rockstar.

When not on the road, JR and I divided our time between NYC and New Jersey. His daughter-in-law gave birth to a second son, whom I happily watched for hours, spellbound. We bought the three-year-old grandson a Superman costume, which he refused to take off, even though it badly needed washing. "NO!" he screamed when I told him it needed to be washed. I asked why, and he said, "Because I'll lose all my magic powers."

"No, you won't," I said. "Your magic powers are in your heart." He was having none of it. His mother finally persuaded him to part with the outfit for an hour. I loved being part of that family.

Then, in 2015, not even a year after our marriage, I developed horrible pains in my abdomen, much worse than the ones two years earlier. The ER doctor diagnosed it as acute pancreatitis, but an endoscopy biopsy revealed a new cancer. My pancreatic surgeon suggested a complete pancreatectomy and splenectomy. "This way, you'll never have to go through another pancreas operation again," he said.

Pancreatic cancer accounts for more than 7 percent of all cancer deaths, and only one in ten survives five years. Since the Whipple,

I'd been reading every obituary in *The New York Times*, shocked there were so many pancreatic cancer deaths, including Ruth Bader Ginsburg, Steve Jobs, Patrick Swayze, and Alex Trebek. I knew I could die, but I didn't go through the "why me" stage because my mother had died of cancer, and it was in my DNA. I gave Lynne the keys to my co-op, changed my will, and called my friends to say hello (I was really calling to say goodbye, but never told them I was about to have a life-threatening operation).

The recovery from the pancreatectomy was much more painful than that from the Whipple. I could barely move and was on a morphine drip. It felt as though someone had twisted sharp arrowheads into my stomach. The surgeon explained that the operation would turn me into a type 1 diabetic (which happens when you have no pancreas and can no longer produce insulin). Right after I was awake, a nurse came into my room with a glucose-testing kit, insulin, and a syringe. She taught me how to prick my finger and take a reading of my blood sugar, calculate how many carbs I planned to eat, figure out how much insulin I needed to cover the carbs, measure out the insulin, and jab the sharp pen into my stomach.

I couldn't stop crying because I hated everything about diabetes, and now I was stuck with it for life. I cried when I forced myself to walk with my IV pole down the corridor, saying over and over: "Move a muscle, stop the pain." The pain didn't stop. Lynne and Howard came to visit, and JR sat with me for days, but everything hurt too much to enjoy their visits. I was disappointed that none of JR's kids came or even called, but maybe they were respecting my privacy. This time, JR made me a very special toy truck and filled the cargo bed with my favorite thing—a raw cotton stem.

I tried to be upbeat but couldn't. When I was finally released, JR went back to New Jersey, and I rehired the nurse I had for the Whipple. Our first walk was two blocks away to my favorite pocket park. The next day, we increased it four blocks to Katharine Hepburn's bench at Dag Hammarskjöld Plaza. Once, we climbed down a long flight of stone steps to a playground on Forty-Ninth Street, but I was too weak to get on the swings. Another time, we walked ten blocks to Forty-Second Street to look at the revolving *Daily News* globe, featured as part of the *Daily Planet* in early Superman films. Two weeks later, the nurse said I didn't need her anymore and should save my money. Seven weeks later, I was finally out of pain, but the diabetes was making me depressed. Surely there had to be a better way to manage it than sticking and jabbing myself four to six times a day.

When I told my MSKCC endocrinologist I wanted to go on a clinical trial, he sent me to Dr. Jason Baker, the superstar endocrinologist at Weill Cornell. Of course, you don't just call Dr. Baker and get an appointment. Even though my endo at MSKCC had put in a good word for me, I had to call Baker's office day after day for weeks before they could finally schedule me. Unfortunately, Dr. Baker said there was no such thing as a diabetes clinical trial. He suggested I wear a continuous glucose monitor on my arm (the size of half a grape) and a tubeless pump below it (the size of half a plum) to deliver insulin. It was a much better solution than constantly sticking myself with needles.

It is now nine years since I've been a type 1 diabetic, and I assure you, it is not for the meek. If I get stressed, eat too many carbs, or work out too hard, my blood glucose, whose ideal number is 120, can skyrocket to 350 and beyond. If I'm not eating enough carbs or I work out too hard (yes, I can go either high or low from exercise), my blood glucose spirals down to a dangerous 70 or below, forcing me to drink juice or eat candy fast. The numbers go up, the numbers go down. It's a constant roller coaster. Worse, often at night, my monitor wakes me up from a deep sleep by beeping, telling me I'm going much too low and have to eat sugar fast. I am so lucky to be a patient of Dr. Baker, because he always has my back, even when I call him late at night, freaked out because my blood sugar has shot up to 450 (usually an occluded pump). Without him, I would be unable to deal with this pernicious disease.

But also, the good news is diabetes cemented my relationship with Lynne. During the Whipple and chemo, it wasn't until I was back to normal that she stopped calling daily. But since the pancreatectomy, she phones every single night to make sure I'm alive. I always tell her I'm fine, but she says, "You have diabetes, and I don't want you dying." She needn't worry. I plan to live to old age, and while I detest everything about diabetes, at least I have a sister who truly cares and loves me.

I finally accepted my diabetes, and life couldn't have been better. I was writing up a storm, had a husband who adored me, and I was back to working out and playing harmonica. But then something horrible and completely unexpected happened, which made having diabetes look like kids' stuff.

25

Marital Problems and More Health Issues

About six months after the pancreatectomy, JR's daughter, who owned his house in New Jersey, decided to sell it to avoid paying two mortgages. JR moved into a much nicer sun-filled apartment with a gym and pool that cost three thousand a month, and which his daughter paid. We continued to commute to both our places until one day JR said, "Look, we don't know how many years we might live, but going forward, we should be living together."

I loved JR but didn't want a full-time live-in. I needed my space. I wasn't about to move into his place, either, so I suggested he spend a few more weeknights in NYC. He said if he spent more time away, his daughter would pay him less, and he'd have money problems.

"Why would you suddenly have money problems?" I asked.

"Because she wants me to pay the three thousand a month for my rent."

This was new. Did she think now that JR and I were married, I would pay his rent?

I said, "Well, how about she pays one thousand a month and you pay the other two thousand from your social security?"

"I guess so," he said. And that was the end of the discussion.

We continued to travel for my assignments, including a motorcycle trip from San Francisco to Yosemite and Lake Tahoe. The scenic route we chose turned every day into a six-hour drive. It was August, and the sun bore down on my heavy helmet and protective gear. Maybe it was stress from the endless driving or stress causing my blood sugar to rise, but I was cranky about everything.

The last day, we drove from Yosemite to Reno to drop off the motorcycle and to catch a 10 p.m. plane back to New York. The drive to Reno was the longest day by far, and it was both hot and exhausting. I was so tired from sitting on the back of the bike that I didn't even care about the gorgeous scenery. I just wanted the ride to be over.

Finally, we drove into the BMW motorcycle dealership and returned the bike. JR said we should take our duffel bags and explore Reno for the next few hours. I had no intention of dragging my heavy bag anywhere and suggested we get a motel room at the airport. JR argued that paying for a room was a waste of money because we'd only be there four hours. What did he care? I was paying! We continued to quarrel, but I wouldn't give in, so we checked into the motel.

After dinner, we still had three hours to kill. JR said we needed to be at the gate two hours in advance. I said that was ridiculous, it was a tiny airport and we'd just be sitting there when we could be resting comfortably here watching TV. He was adamant, so we finally compromised on one hour in advance at the airport, even though he continued to say one hour was too late. At 9 p.m., we walked across the street to the airport. There was no one else there. Our gate wasn't even open. JR sat at the gate, and I chose a massage chair two gates away, feeding it every dollar I had. I was still so furious, even the kneading chair didn't calm me down. Finally, we boarded, but by the time we landed in New York, we were still livid with each other. Normally, JR would have spent the night, but he went home to New Jersey instead. A few days later, we both got over our anger, but things were corroding. We hadn't even been married a year.

One night, he said, "Look, we're married, and it's ridiculous we aren't living together. I should move in with you."

This was the *last* thing I wanted, but I didn't know how to say no. I loved him, and he'd always been there for me, especially day after day at the hospital for both operations. I hid my resentment and told him to move in, but said he should keep his apartment because it had a pool and was a grandkid magnet. Secretly, I was hoping he would just move in temporarily and then move back home.

At first, it was fine. He did the shopping, cooked the meals, and was quiet when we read the paper in our respective chairs. After breakfast, I'd disappear into my study, close the door, and write. Still, I wasn't used to having a man in my living room, as I'd been alone well over ten years. When I passed through to the kitchen, JR would be in his chair asleep, mouth wide open, snoring.

I soon hated the arrangement and began to resent paying for all the groceries, restaurant meals, his gas, the NYC parking garage, airline tickets, theatre tickets, and more. He sat around all day and did nothing but watch TV and nap. I hadn't signed up for a house husband, I'd signed up for a weekend partner/lover and someone with whom to travel.

One night, out of nowhere, he asked, "When are you going to pay the twelve thousand you said you would?"

My fork dropped. "*What* twelve thousand?"

"When we talked about spending more time together, I told you my daughter would pay me less, and I asked you to pay two thousand a month for my rent. It's been six months. You said you'd pay it out of your social security."

"I said *what*?"

"You said you'd pay two thousand a month," he said.

"I would never say such a thing," I said. "And if I did say that, why would you wait six months to bring it up?"

"Because I was embarrassed. I was hoping you would step up to what you said you'd do," he said.

"But I never said that!" I insisted. "I would never keep a man."

"Who paid for your country house and your last apartment?" he said.

"Jack," I said.

"So?" he said. "What's the difference?"

"For one thing," I said, "I was brought up that the man pays, and why would I want to increase my monthly maintenance by two thousand dollars?"

We argued for days. He moved back to his place in New Jersey. I phoned him and said this was like *Rashomon* and it would always be a he said/she said. I told him I loved him and wanted him back.

"How do we get back to where we were before this happened?" I asked.

He said that for us to go forward, we had to come together and pay for everything as a union, and that he knew I'd be resentful.

"Look," he said, "your perceptions regarding a man's role in a marriage are deep-rooted and fixed. Given these concerns, I don't see a way forward."

I didn't want to lose him, but I didn't want to have to pay his rent, either. We were at a standstill.

He said, "We went into this marriage as two people in love, and I thought we had the intent to join and unite as partners."

I knew his daughter must have instigated this, because never before had he brought up this partnership thing.

"You knew I had no money," he said, "but I felt you recognized I bring other assets to our marriage. Your goal of marriage is different from my perception. It doesn't make sense to bump along."

He was adamant. I persuaded him to come with me to a couple's therapist. She asked why JR had no money and he admitted he'd lost eight million dollars in a partnership deal.

"Didn't you have a contract?" she asked.

He said he'd done the deal on a handshake. She looked at him in disbelief.

"You are very naïve about money," she said. Then she turned to me. "And you are very controlling. If you two expect to work this out, you're going to have to spend an awful lot of time talking through it."

I thought JR would spend the night, but he went back to New Jersey.

Maybe I'd been so blindsided by my health issues that I hadn't been thinking clearly, but I didn't want a traditional marriage or a full-time relationship. Still, I loved him and didn't want to lose him. He'd never lied to me and wouldn't have made this up, so maybe I *had* agreed to pay the two thousand dollars. If I were to pay, I wouldn't go broke, so what was the big deal? I called him and asked, "Besides the two thousand a month, what do you need from me to make this work?"

"We have to be partners going forward," he said. "I'd need to study your financial statements and make suggestions."

"*What?*" I said. This was absurd.

"I want to understand how your financial advisor is doing with your portfolio. What kind of returns he's getting on an annual basis."

"My financial advisor is doing fine," I said. "I don't need help."

"I want to make sure you don't have a Bernie Madoff situation," he said. "Equal partners do things together. Each party looks out for the other."

This was never going to work for me. "Look," I said, "I love you, but let's get a divorce and see each other only on the weekends, the way we used to."

He wouldn't agree.

I knew I'd hurt him horribly, but I wasn't about to share my financial statements and have him make decisions—not from a guy who'd lost eight million dollars on a handshake. I called Jack and told him I was getting a divorce.

He said, "Marriage is like a roach motel. It's easy to get into and almost impossible to get out of."

Jack wasn't wrong. JR's lawyer demanded I pay twelve thousand for the six months of rent. I objected, so the divorce dragged on for months. I felt really badly and guilty, and just in case I *had* said I'd pay two thousand, I gave him six, half of what he'd asked for. When the divorce was finalized, I had to pay both his lawyer and mine. Wasted money.

Back to being alone, it was time to find some joy. I started doing MMA with a trainer twice a week (which I loved, because I could smack his mitts as hard as possible and never get hit back). I returned to the Shack Up Inn and Jam Camp in Clarksdale. I discovered two more open-mic jams in NYC, and along with Big Ed's Famous Blues Jam Monday nights, I now had open-mic jams every Wednesday and Saturday night. I spent more time hanging out with friends and continued to travel for stories. I returned to *Travel Classics*, this time in Ireland, where, besides pitching top editors, I became good friends with Maren Rudolph (the founder) and Ruth Moran of *Tourism Ireland*. It wasn't just at the conference. We got together back in New York City, often laughing so hard our sides ached. Happily, our unique and wonderful friendship continues to this day. Having a man in my life was no longer my priority. I was healthy again, and had friends, workout buddies, and open-mic jams.

One day, I saw my oncologist on a routine visit after my biannual MRI, and she told me there was an increased nodule in my lower right lung. We could wait to see if it grew, biopsy it, or take it out. No way was I waiting. "Take it out," I said, hoping it was the last errant pancreas cell and not the beginning of ongoing lung cancer. The week before the operation, I tried to mask my fear. That Monday night at the Red Lion, Christine Santelli, who co-runs Big Ed's jam and is a good friend, hugged me hello, and I burst out crying. I told her I might have lung cancer. She tried to console me, but I couldn't stop the tears because so few people survive lung cancer.

I said goodbye to my friends (who again thought I was calling to say hello) and prepared for the worst. Lynne and Howard accompanied me to the hospital. I hadn't told JR about the operation because we hadn't spoken since the divorce. Lynne was with me in the cubicle when I changed into the gown. She'd always hated the sound of the harmonica (I have no idea why), and not once in the eight years I'd been playing had she ever come to a jam to hear me, not even on my birthday. Now she was my captive prisoner.

When the nurse came to take me into the operating room, I whipped out my harp and played the most soulful version of "Amazing Grace" I could. Lynne cried, and then I cried. It might be the last song I ever played. MSKCC's skillful thoracic surgeon took out a portion of my lower right lobe, arthroscopically. When I woke up, it hurt to talk, it hurt to breathe, and it hurt to move an inch. If I took too big a bite of food, I'd cough uncontrollably and would have to call for the nurse to pound her fists on my back to make it stop. As the nurse never answered right away, I coughed until my throat was raw.

They gave me a spirometer to measure my air capacity; I was to breathe, and a little ball would climb up the tube. It was almost impossible because I kept coughing. And it wasn't just me; the soundtrack of the entire thoracic ward was nonstop hacking. No one walked the corridors because everyone was in bed, coughing. I was *not* going to let this beat me, so I forced myself out of bed. Tubes were attached to my back and the side of my chest. My bandage pulled like a much-too-tight corset. I gasped in pain with every step, but made myself walk the halls. And then, I discovered the patient lounge.

My roommate, who'd also had a lobe removed, was lovely but had a constant parade of family members visiting and talking nonstop. I grabbed my harmonica, went to the lounge, closed my eyes, and warbled out a blues tune. It was so much more satisfying than blowing into the spirometer.

"Wanna jam?" said a male voice. I opened my eyes. The music therapist was standing there with his guitar. Was I dreaming? We played a slow blues shuffle. At the end of the song, a gaggle of doctors and nurses stood in the doorway, applauding. Granted, I wasn't that good, but considering the circumstances, I felt like Stevie Wonder.

The recovery was long and painful. Again, I hired the private nurse, and we walked the streets until I was ready to be on my own. One day, I went to Central Park. In the past, I'd always run and ride my bike, training for a marathon or triathlon. Now, I could only walk slowly. And to my complete surprise, it was extremely soothing wandering the North Woods listening to the waterfalls and looking up, hoping to see an owl or a red-tailed hawk.

I sold my triathlon bike because I didn't want to pedal that fast anymore. Instead, I rode a Citi Bike. I continued to do MMA with my fabulous trainer, but shorter intervals. (I still box and lift weights with him twice a week.) After a few months, I was back to normal. Everyone thought it was incredible that I'd recovered so quickly, but the secret is simple—keep moving even when it hurts. I'd once again beaten the grim reaper, but what I didn't know was that I was about to come the closest I ever have to death.

26

My Life Today

I returned to my normal life and began to travel again. Even though I wrote every day, I often wondered if my writing was good enough (what writer doesn't?). Then, I remembered my interview with Francis Ford Coppola, who told me, "I think I wasn't born with a talent to write, and I struggle all the time overcoming that lack of a gift through hard work. Writing, like acting, is something you can get better and better and even get good at through effort."

I knew he'd always been a risk-taker and asked him how that ethic came about. He said, "I think somewhere I got the idea that when you live your life, the only way you could really fail would be if you were some old guy dying saying, 'Oh! I wish I had done that, and I wish I had done this.' When I pass away, I basically have nothing I wish I had done, because I did it all. I did everything I wanted to do and continue to live that way."

Me too. Throughout my childhood and teens, fear stopped me from trying anything new. But by my twenties, I finally learned to be afraid of nothing, including playing harmonica in public. I know I'm not a great musician, but I've learned that playing with a band is about serving the song, not my ego. I've made good friends at that jam, and there's nothing better than having friends.

With my back-to-normal life, I stopped thinking about meeting a guy. And then, out of the blue, a really good guitar player to whom I'd never spoken other than saying hello (because he only seemed to speak guitar) approached me at a jam and asked me to dinner. During dinner, he admitted he'd asked me out because I had such an easy way with people, and he did not. He told me he and his last girlfriend had gone on vacation to Maine. She wanted to visit a different town every day, and he preferred to stay in one place. That was the opposite of me, so obviously this would never work. Still, he could talk about much more than just guitar, and it was nice to be in someone's arms again. We started staying with each other on weekends.

I was assigned a story on Chicago, and knowing it would be just one hotel, asked if he wanted to come. Happily, he paid for his own airline ticket. The Chicago Tourism Bureau had sent a long list of activities from an architectural river tour to a barbeque festival. I figured he wouldn't want to do too much, but he told me he wanted to do everything. Maybe he was my kind of guy after all. But when we arrived in Chicago and raced from the river tour to the 360 Observation Deck to the BBQ festival, he complained it was too much, and we should cancel much of the next day. I explained we'd committed to these activities, and it would be rude to change the schedule. He sulked. He sighed. He scowled. He was a Type C. I'm Type A. This would never work. When we arrived back in New York, he walked out of my life as quickly as he'd walked in. But I didn't really care, because my life was full without him.

One night, I woke up at 2 a.m. with blood all over my sheets. I felt so weak and dizzy I could barely get out of bed, dial 911, crawl to my front door, unlock it, and collapse on the floor. In my brownstone, the doormen work from 8 a.m. to midnight, but each apartment has a buzzer for the off hours. I heard my buzzer ring but was too weak to buzz in EMS. The phone rang. I could hear a voice saying, "Hello? Hello? Is this Margie Goldsmith? This is EMS. We can't get in." I couldn't move. I lay on the ground knowing if I couldn't let them in, I might die.

I took deep breaths and tried to stay awake. Finally, I heard voices in the hallway. Saved! The EMS team had mistakenly buzzed my neighbor, Kathryne Lyons, and she led them upstairs. With my blood pressure now 80/60, they lifted me onto a gurney. Kathryne insisted on following the ambulance to the hospital. It was almost 2:30 a.m. I told her to go home, but she said, "I'm not leaving you all alone." It was the greatest act of kindness and generosity I have ever experienced, especially from someone I barely knew. The ER doctor explained I had a bleeding ulcer (one of the Whipple clamps had broken free). They put in a new clamp and gave me a blood transfusion. I begged Kathryne to go home, but she refused to leave. At 4 a.m. I demanded she go home. She literally saved my life.

After a few days and a few more transfusions, I was back home. And just then, COVID hit. Life was cancelled. No more jams, no more indoor dining, no more friendly get-togethers. I had to mask up every time I left the house or went downstairs for the mail. I wiped down every grocery bag. Each night at 7 p.m., everyone in my neighborhood would throw open their windows and bang on pots and pans to honor the healthcare workers. I faced my amplifier toward the window, pulled out my harmonica, and played "When the Saints Go Marching In."

The pandemic continued, and everyone was miserable and bored, but I wasn't because I was used to being alone. I kept on writing, doing interviews on Zoom instead of in person. Every morning, I'd unlock a Citi Bike, wipe down the handlebars, and head to Central Park. The streets were so empty I could bike through every red light, including on Park Avenue. Central Park was empty too. It was as though I owned the city.

Because I wasn't traveling, I had more time on my hands, so I wrote a nonfiction book, *Masters of the Harmonica: 30 Master Harmonica Players Share Their Craft*. I was used to interviewing CEOs and celebrities, but I was intimidated interviewing these top harmonica virtuosos because they were (and are) my harmonica idols: Rick Estrin, Joe Filisko, Dennis Gruenling, Jason Ricci, Charlie Musselwhite, Magic Dick, Kim Wilson, Delbert McClinton, Charlie McCoy—thirty of the best harmonica players performing today.

By the time the book was published, the pandemic was still going strong. I'd been alone for months and ached for company. Then I learned about Muddy Paws, an organization that lets you foster a dog for a few weeks before it finds a "forever" home. I could never permanently have a dog, because who would take care of it if I had another hospital emergency or was traveling? But having one for a few weeks sounded perfect.

Lisa, who was part terrier and part beagle, greeted me each morning by jumping onto my bed. I was in love. Sometimes, I wondered if she was just playing me or merely looking for a snack, but even after a few days, she licked my face and hands. When I took her outside, she never pulled at her leash, never barked, did her business in a timely manner, and sat willingly on each street corner until I said we could cross.

By day six, she looked at me with such love, I thought my heart would burst. She was a Velcro dog and followed me everywhere. She lay on the bathmat when I took a shower. She jumped onto my lap if I was reading the newspaper. If I was on a Zoom call, she'd watch. No man had ever been this attentive. But when I practiced harmonica, she tilted her head and ran out of the room. Was I that bad? The problem with Lisa was she couldn't discuss the news or hold a conversation or tell me why she didn't like my harmonica playing. She wasn't like a mate, she was more like a baby who needed constant care, with walks five times a day, including at night. After two weeks, Muddy Paws called. Did I want Lisa as my forever dog? Because if not, someone wanted her. I gave Lisa one last kiss and delivered her to her new forever owner.

COVID continued. I needed a new project to inspire me. I continued to write articles, but also began to write songs, encouraged by my harmonica teacher, from whom I took Skype lessons each week. After I'd written ten songs, I decided to make an album, but I needed a producer and band. I thought about the harmonica players I'd interviewed. Who would be most fun to record with? Rick Estrin, of course, who plays harmonica, sings, and fronts the band Rick Estrin and the Nightcats. I'd also seen his hysterical video in which he says, "You play a riff and put your head down and shake it as if you're saying, 'Damn, that shit is deep.'" I called Rick. How does a non-pro like me get to record with the hottest blues band in America? You ask. What's the worst they can do? Say no. Much to my shock, Rick agreed to co-produce my album with Kid Andersen, guitarist/producer/engineer. We'd do it at Kid's studio, Greaseland, in San Jose. A lot of hit records have come out of there.

Not only did Rick give me great advice about making every word better, but the talented musicians with whom I recorded made every song sing—Rick on harp (I played some too), Kid on guitar and engineer, D'mar Martin on drums, Lorenzo Farrell on keys, and Randy Bermudes on bass. There's nothing these guys can't do, and I was so happy with the album I put out, *Margie Goldsmith and Friends*, on Spotify.

When COVID finally waned, Rick Estrin and the Nightcats came to New York City, and we debuted the album publicly at the Bitter End in the Village. The experience was so uplifting that the following year I wrote ten new songs, returned to Greaseland, and recorded the album. The band returned to New York City, and we played the new album, *Margie Goldsmith & Friends Part 2*, at the Bitter End. I thought about writing ten new songs and doing a

Part 3 with the same talented guys, but I'm not pushing myself. If the songs materialize, fine. If not, I don't really care.

I think that's the best thing about aging—you don't have to prove anything anymore. You can slow down a little. Of course, considering the roller coaster ride of my life, I don't want to slow down too much, because I want to pack in as much as possible with whatever time I have left. The main thing is I try to live as a "yes" person rather than a "no" person. I've been to 150 countries and have won 101 writing awards, but in the end, what does that mean? Nothing. What truly matters is my relationships with my friends, who continue to uplift me, even with my ongoing health issues.

A year ago, I had a total knee replacement. The surgery went fine, but the PT had me doing things too soon, which resulted in a hematoma and a second operation, followed by a Baker's cyst, which burst and set me back to ground zero. It has now been eighteen months, and the knee is still wonky. I can't walk more than a mile without having to rest, and because my balance is off, I wouldn't dare ride a bike outside. I accept the fact that I will never be an outdoor athlete again, but I still box with a trainer, lift weights, and ride my road bike indoors on a bike trainer.

But there's one thing I don't stop thinking about. If I were to die, what would I have given back? Each of my operations could have killed me, yet I was always saved by brilliant surgeons who had obviously learned about the human body by working on cadavers. And then I knew what I could give back—my corpse.

I made an appointment with the Chief of Gross Anatomy at Weill Cornell, who took me into a room full of corpses hidden under thick, green plastic tarps. His assistant rolled back a tarp revealing a cadaver about eighty years old, a man with whiskers. I asked who he was, and the chief said they only knew his name was Joe. Joe looked healthy. Maybe they wouldn't want a body so surgically repaired. I told the chief I'd had a Whipple, had no pancreas, was missing a lobe of my lung, had no spleen, no gallbladder, no ovaries, and a Titanium knee. Would that disqualify me?

"Oh, not at all," he said. "It would be an excellent learning tool for medical students."

When I signed the papers of consent, I asked them to attach a note to my cadaver. I didn't want to be just Margie the way the guy with the whiskers was just Joe. The note reads:

My name was Margie Goldsmith. I lived my life as freely as I could, even though hindered by recurring cancer, an ulcer bleed, and eighteen hospital visits. I tried as many new activities as I could and traveled the world during my lifetime. I loved every place I visited and every person I met. If you're afraid to travel, as I was at first, just take a deep breath and go anyway. Go everywhere. Go where you don't speak the language, go where you're out of your comfort zone. Both traveling and trying new activities, especially those that scared me, made me a more compassionate, happier person. May they do the same for you.

Now you know all about me. Hopefully, it has inspired you to go for what you want and not settle for anything less—whether a relationship or a career. And if you happen to be considering marriage, please discuss money before you say yes. But above all, say yes to life, because it really goes by fast. I used to remember every day of every week. Now, it feels as though I go from Sunday to Thursday in one day and have no idea where the time went or what I even did on those days. Maybe that happens to everyone as they age. But if you live your life as "someday I'll do this," then you won't do anything. I have always lived my life like the old Nike ad, "Just do it." So far, I've beaten the grim reaper four times, and I plan to keep kicking his butt, because I don't give in. I've become a badass. Now, you go be one too.

THE END

Acknowledgments

Thank you to everyone who was kind enough to read this book during its long developmental phase, especially Judy Kirkwood (who read it multiple times), Lynne Miller (my sister and biggest fan), Sue Cohen, Sherri Suib Cohen, Maren Rudolph, and Ruth Moran. And thank you so much to Patrick Perry, Jeff Berger, and Lee Woodruff, who allowed me to use their comments. Special thanks to Susie Stangland and Lauren Beck. I thank the indomitable superstar doctors who have kept me alive since my first health scare in 2014: at Memorial Sloane Kettering Cancer Center— Dr. Eileen O'Reilly, Dr. William Jarnagin, and Dr. Matthew Bott; at Weill Cornell Medical Center—Dr. Jason Baker, Dr. Carl Crawford, and Dr. Costas Hanjis; and at Hospital for Special Surgery—Dr. Marci Goolsby. I am truly grateful that all of you have made it possible for me to charge ahead full steam. Special thanks to my wellness team: Chris Aronsen and Andrea Nieto.

About the Author

Margie Goldsmith, author of two non-fiction books and a novel, began her career as an apprentice for Joe Papp at the New York Shakespeare Festival. Upon college graduation, she left for Paris and remained for the next four years, developing her film skills and writing a novel. Four years later, she returned to New York City and worked as the writer/director/ producer of a film production company before opening MG Productions LLC. Ten years later, she sold her company in order to travel the world with a pen and notebook as a freelance writer. Since then, she has visited 150 countries on seven continents and written over 1,000 magazine and newspaper articles. She has won 101 creative writing awards, including an Emmy for a TV documentary, "The Holy Shroud of Turin." Physical activity is her passion, and Goldsmith has completed marathons and Olympic distance triathlons, summited Mount Rainier, and climbed to Advanced Base Camp on the north face of Mount Everest. Goldsmith plays blues harmonica and has recorded two albums as a singer/songwriter/harmonica player: *Margie Goldsmith & Friends Part I and Part 2*. She continues to travel the world and always brings harmonicas to both play and give away.

Also by
Margie Goldsmith

Masters of the Harmonica: 30 Master Harmonica Players Share Their Craft

Alice Dalton Browne: Nocturnes and Diurnes. Recent Paintings

Screwup

www.ingramcontent.com/pod-product-compliance
Lightning Source LLC
Chambersburg PA
CBHW052137070526
44585CB00017B/1860